How to Teach Your Dyslexic Child to Read

How to Teach Your Dyslexic Child to Read

A Proven Method for Parents and Teachers

Bernice H. Baumer

Illustrations by Melanie Trendelman

Citadel Press
Kensington Publishing Corp.
www.kensingtonbooks.com

CITADEL PRESS books are published by

Kensington Publishing Corp.
850 Third Avenue
New York, NY 10022

All Kensington titles, imprints, and distributed lines are available at special quantity discounts for bulk purchases for sales promotions, premiums, fund raising, educational, or institutional use. Special book excerpts or customized printings can also be created to fit specific needs. For details, write or phone the office of the Kensington special sales manager: Kensington Publishing Corp., 850 Third Avenue, New York, NY 10022, attn: Special Sales Department, phone 1-800-221-2647.

Kensington and the K logo Reg. U.S. Pat. & TM Office
Citadel Press is a trademark of Kensington Publishing Corp.

First printing 1998

10 9 8 7 6 5 4 3 2

Printed in the United States of America

Library of Congress Cataloging-in-Publication Data

Baumer, Bernice H.
    How to teach your dyslexic child to read : a proven method for parents and teachers / Bernice H. Baumer ; illustrations by Melanie Trendelman.
        p.   cm.
    "A Citadel Press book."
    Originally published: 1996
    ISBN 0-8065-1981-9 (pbk.)
    1. Dyslexic children—Education—United States.   2. Reading (Elementary)—United States.   I. Title
[LC4709.B386   1998]
371.91'44—dc21   98-9399
                                                          CIP

Contents

Part 3
Pictures, Charts, and Word Lists You Can Use
to Teach Your Child to Read

Preface

Many children find learning to read very easy—not so the dyslexics. Without one-to-one help many find it very difficult.

For more than twenty-five years I have been tutoring dyslexics, teaching them to read. I have seen discouraged boys and girls blossom. Each child I tutored has taught me something. I feel that every child of average intelligence or above can learn to read if he is taught by a parent or tutor who knows how to teach him. The dyslexic's parents can successfully teach him to read if they have the proper materials, know-how, and enough love and stick-to-itiveness to faithfully tutor him a half hour or hour day after day.

This book has three parts: In Part One learning disabilities problems are discussed. Each problem is followed by a true story of how a child was helped to overcome that disability.

Part Two tells how to teach the dyslexic to read, step by step, from kindergarten through the first, second, and third grades. It also gives detailed instructions for teaching phonics, spelling, and syllabication.

Part Three contains the pictures, charts, and word lists parents and tutors will need when teaching the child to read.

WHO IS DYSLEXIC?

It is impossible to tell if a child is dyslexic by just looking at him. How can a parent or a teacher decide that a child needs one-to-one tutoring?

In their first four months of school, most first graders develop a basic word vocabulary that enables them to begin reading sentences. However, usually there are two or three children out of every ten who cannot accomplish this. There are various reasons for a child being unable to keep up with his peers:

1. He may have missed necessary learning skills because of absence due to illness.

2. He may be a slow starter with no problem other than being slow in maturing.
3. His intelligence level may be below average.
4. He may have such a short attention span (ADD, attention deficit disorder) that it is impossible for him to listen to most of his teacher's instructions.
5. He may be a dyslexic.

Teachers are confronted with the difficult task of locating the reason for each child's lack of success and setting in motion a program that will correct it. If a first grader is falling far behind by the middle of first grade, one-to-one teaching may save him from acquiring a reading disability.

Worried parents ask teachers, "Is my child a dyslexic? He's making letters and numbers backward."

Dyslexia is a lack of coordination between sight and sound. It is a generalized disturbance of language function that interferes with the acquisition of reading skills. Webster defines dyslexia as "a disturbance of the ability to read."

Many young children reverse the letters b, d, p, and q. Reversing letters and numbers is usually dropped by normal children before the end of the second grade. Some dyslexics continue to make letters backward and confuse the directions of left and right.

Caution should be used in labeling children dyslexic, especially in the first two grades. Many children are just slow starters who, with proper instruction, will have no persistent reading problems.

Being a dyslexic would not be a problem in a nonliterate society. In all areas except reading he may perform very well, but reading is necessary in today's literate world.

Dyslexia varies in degree of severity. There are clues that indicate a child may be a dyslexic, but because each individual is different, every child will not have the same problems. Very often young dyslexics who receive one-to-one year-round tutoring are able to make normal progress in regular classrooms by the time they reach third grade.

A major clue indicating dyslexia is slow word recall. Initially a dyslexic may be able to learn required words, then seem to deteriorate because he is unable to retrieve his expanded reading vocabulary. The dyslexic may read slowly because he finds it hard to recall the words he has learned. He may say a word correctly in one paragraph and then hesitate when trying to recall it in the next. Often he substitutes a synonym for a word he's trying to recall; street may be road; house, home; and pail, bucket. Another major clue of dyslexia is when a child has average or above intelligence and is reading two or more years below his peers when he is in the third grade or beyond.

Many dyslexics continue to reverse and invert letters and transpose words. They have difficulty distinguishing between b and d, p and d or b, g and d or b. To them, words with these initial sounds are more confusing when they occur in word lists than when they are in sentences. Did may be bib; lip, lid; ripe, ride; god, dog; and pat, bat. They often say saw for was, and felt for left.

The dyslexic has more difficulty retrieving grammar words than content words. Frequently he mispronounces words such as of, for, what, and that. His visual memory for words seems to play an insignificant role in word recognition.

The dyslexic finds it hard to live with being called stupid. He may be miserable at school and become a problem child, or he may withdraw into himself. Having a serious dyslexic repeat a grade will probably accomplish nothing. It may make him feel even more discouraged. However, with the right type of one-to-one tutoring he can be taught to read.

Each dyslexic is different. The teacher or tutor must, through careful observation, determine how to structure the dyslexic's lessons. Which is his strongest learning channel—auditory, visual, or kinesthetic? Will a combination of two or all of these channels be most helpful? Does this child have a short attention span? By a combination of activities can it be lengthened? What is his learning pace? After a phonics concept has been introduced, how much drill and review will be necessary for him to understand and use it? How many vocabulary words should he be asked to learn at one time—four, five, or six? How many pages should be assigned for daily oral reading—two, three, or four? How many words can he learn to spell in a week and remember how to spell when writing sentences?

Daily reading aloud provides the dyslexic child with the word repetition he needs to develop quick word recall. Reading silently is of little help when he is struggling to recall words.

If the child is asked to read stories that are too difficult, he may become frustrated and discouraged. Stories should be selected carefully, and gradually stepped up in difficulty. The child should know ninety-five percent of the words in a story, and before he is asked to read it, flash cards should be used to teach him the new words he will encounter.

A child who is constantly hesitating to recall words may get little meaning from the paragraph he is reading. If, after he reads the paragraph, his tutor reads it aloud with expression and then asks him to reread it, the child's comprehension will improve.

The child should always be encouraged to talk about what is happening in a story. Questions such as "How do you think this story will end, and why?" will help the child develop cognitive learning.

The dyslexic can learn whole words, but he has trouble recalling them. Because drills and frequent reviews are necessary for him to expand his vocabulary, phonetic skills are keys to his success. These should be taught step by step in a logical order. Many repetitious one-to-one drills in the use of each skill are usually required to teach the child to use that skill automatically.

There are a great many phonetic rules. Teaching all of them would confuse the child, take too much time, and bore him. The necessary rules are discussed in developmental order in this book. Properly taught, these rules, together with instruction in syllabication, will provide the dyslexic with the tools he needs to learn and recall words.

One-to-one reading should continue until the child is able to read fluently (it may be slowly) and comprehend at third-grade level or above. If the child then continues to read for pleasure on his own a half hour each day, he may very well become one of the "compensated dyslexics" who need no special help in furthering their education.

Researchers say five to ten percent of the children in school are dyslexics, and more boys are diagnosed dyslexic than girls. This may be because the typical cognitive profile for girls is that they are better at verbal skills than spacial skills, while boys are better at spacial than verbal skills. Girls may be more inclined to compensate for their difficulty in learning to read. Once they have managed to learn a few words, they may develop compensatory strategies that will help them minimize their reading weakness. Also, while boys are engaging in active sports, girls may be improving their word recall on their own by daily reading.

Blue eyes and brown eyes are inherited. It appears that dyslexia is also inherited. Most dyslexics have at least one relative (a sibling, father, mother, uncle, aunt, or cousin) who has had difficulty learning to read.

A recent study was made of eleven three-generation families in an effort to detect the effects of the gene or genes leading to dyslexia, and there were dyslexics in every generation of these families. The findings indicated that there were no more dyslexics in these families that were left-handed or had allergies than there were in nondyslexic families. Approximately the same number of males and females were dyslexic; however, dyslexia in the males was more severe.[1]

The dyslexic child must be encouraged to read a few pages each day, and daily reading must become a lifelong habit. Frequently adult dyslexics lose their word-recall skills if they do very little reading.

Encourage the child by telling him about famous dyslexics. Leonardo da Vinci (1452–1519), the artist who painted *Mona Lisa*, recorded plans in notebooks for hundreds of inventions including a moveable bridge and a flying machine. All his notes were written backward and could only be read with a mirror.

Albert Einstein (1879–1955) is famous for his theory of relativity, which laid the basis for the release of atomic energy. Einstein did not talk until he was past three.

The American public official Nelson A. Rockefeller (1906–1979) was a dyslexic. He made many contributions to human welfare, served as governor of New York from 1959 to 1973, and was vice president under President Gerald Ford.

The child should be told there are engineers, lawyers, musicians, doctors, university professors, and artists who are dyslexic. He should know

---

1. Lubs, Herbert A., Mark Rabin, Esther Feldman, Bonnie J. Jallad, Alexander Kushch, Karen Gross-Glenn, Ranjan Duara, and R. C. Elston. "Familial Dyslexia: Genetic and Medical Findings in Eleven Three-Generation Families." *Annals of Dyslexia*. The Orton Dyslexia Society, Vol, XLIII, 1993: 44–60.

that being dyslexic will not keep him from being successful in doing whatever he wants.

A group of neuroscientists are studying various aspects of dyslexia in the hope that their research will lead to greater understanding of the development of the brain for cognitive and emotional behavior.[2] They say that learned association is stored in only one hemisphere of the brain and that both hemispheres have access to the stimuli during the learning phase. "In individuals with learning disorders there is a slowing of the development of the left hemisphere and a compensatory growth of the right hemisphere." This may interfere with the brain's normal left-to-right hemisphere balance, and during a learning task may cause the child to make inferior progress.[3]

---

2. This group of neuroscientists first met in Florence, Italy, in 1988, to plan studies on developmental dyslexia. The group was composed of twenty-four neuroscientists from six different nations—England, the Netherlands, Norway, Spain, Switzerland, and the United States. Articles on their studies were published as *Dyslexia and Development* (Harvard University Press, Cambridge, Mass: 1993).

3. Rosin, Glenn D., Gordon F. Sherman, Albert M. Galaburda. "Dyslexia and Brain Pathology" (135–36) *Dyslexia and Development*, edited by M. Galaburda, Harvard University Press, Cambridge, Massachusetts, 1993.

Part 1

Disability Problems and Ways to Correct Them

The Beginners

Reading is an essential skill in today's ever-changing world, and love of reading should be developed before a child enters school. If his parents read stories to him every day, stories that he understands and enjoys, the child will learn to love books and want to learn to read them.

If the parent selects books with many pictures and only a few sentences on each page, by moving his finger beneath the words as he reads, he or she can teach the child that words are read from left to right. Often beginners' reading problems stem from their not knowing this.

The pace at which most first graders learn to read amazes me. Because they have already spent a year in kindergarten, many have learned to recognize the alphabet and know some letter sounds. In their first four months of first grade they learn to read many words. By the end of the school year they have developed a reading vocabulary of perhaps two hundred words. They have also learned to print words and to spell some of them.

However, out of every ten first graders there are usually two, or maybe three, who are unable to accomplish this. Why was a child unable to keep up with his peers? Usually for one of these reasons:

1. He may be a slow learner.
2. He may not have matured enough to listen attentively to the teacher when he or she introduces words and reading skills.
3. He may have been ill and missed too many school days.
4. He may be a dyslexic.

If he is too far behind, it may be necessary for him to repeat first grade, or with tutoring he may still be able to catch up. His teacher may suggest that he attend summer school and promise to have him retested. In either case, this child needs your understanding and help. If he is to repeat first grade, make sure he does not forget the words he has learned. Get preprimers from the public library and help him read them orally. Do not let him guess at words or try to sound them. Tell him the words he doesn't know.

To learn to read, a child must read aloud. He must also say all the words correctly. If he is told to read without help, he will fill in wrong words for those he does not know.

Much of what I know about the teaching of reading I have learned from experience. For many years I have taught dyslexics one-to-one and kept records of their progress. I will tell you about some of these children and their problems. I've changed all their names except Hannah's. Hannah, who has since learned to write very well, gave me permission to use the first story she wrote.

Daily Tutoring

It does not take hours of daily tutoring to bring a child's reading up to grade level. If the child is guided properly, less than an hour of one-to-one daily tutoring works wonders.

Amy

It was springtime when I was asked to tutor Amy. She had scored very low on the first-grade reading tests, and her mother was told Amy would have to repeat first grade.

Amy is a bright little girl, but she is a dyslexic. When she came to see me, she brought two preprimers with her and opened the first, saying, "I can read this one." She had it memorized.

She opened the second preprimer to its first page, saying, "This is a song, I will sing it for you." She turned the first few pages as she sang.

She had not memorized the next page. She looked at it sadly and shook her head. "Reading is not for me," she said. She looked so discouraged my heart went out to her. I said, "Never mind, Amy. You and I will work together, and you will learn to read."

On May 3 I began tutoring Amy one hour each week. I planned her lessons carefully and taught her mother how to tutor her. Every week I made a brief outline, listing what she was to be taught each day. Her mother was to work with her thirty or forty minutes daily.

Amy learned the consonant and vowel sounds, and through daily drill with flash cards, five words at a time, she learned the preprimer's vocabulary words. At the end of the month she took the third preprimer to school. "I can read now," she told her teacher. "I will read for you." Her teacher was very kind. She promised to have Amy retested at the end of summer school.

Amy's parents and I continued tutoring her. She did not have to repeat first grade, and her reading gradually improved. However, because Amy is a dyslexic, she could not have accomplished this without one-to-one tutoring.

Making Letters Backward

A child must not be labeled dyslexic just because he makes letters backward or is not sure of the directions "left" and "right." Many young children make letters backward and do not realize the importance of directions. Perhaps no one has called this to their attention. I believe some children are slightly dyslexic, and others are severely so. With the help of parents and teachers, slightly dyslexic children soon learn to cope with directional problems and do well in school.

Dawn

Dawn, a second grader, knew how to spell every word on spelling tests, but when the teacher gave the test, she left out words and made letters backward. She tried to write each word the teacher pronounced but found this impossible because she had to keep referring to the alphabet strip above the blackboard to see if she was making the letters correctly.

The teacher taped a list of lower-case letters across the top of Dawn's desk. This helped solve her problem. She learned to make letters and numbers correctly and did well in second grade.

Severe dyslexics continue to have directional problems beyond third grade. They may make letters backward and reverse the order of letters when reading words. The word was may be read saw; felt, left; dig, big; put, tub; and gum, mug. Many find b, d, p, and g very confusing.

Using the sense of touch—the tactile approach—is a definite help in teaching a child to distinguish confusing letters. Have him write letters and words with his fingertip in "invisible" writing on a rough surface. The rough side of a 18″ × 24″ masonite board is excellent for such practice.

It can be used with the smooth side up during most of the lesson and then turned over for "invisible" writing.

If the child has difficulty distinguishing between the letters b and d, have him practice only the letter b, saying the sound of b each time he "writes" the letter with his fingertip. Do not practice the letter d. Once he has mastered the direction of the letter b, he will know the letter turned the opposite way is a d.

Even after a child seems to have mastered the form of the letter b, he occasionally becomes confused and needs to practice its shape. On a strip of rough paper, print six large lower-case b's. Ask the child to practice saying the sound of b, or a word with that initial sound, as he traces each b with his fingertip. Use this strip for a few minutes practice each day for a week or so, until he feels sure of its sound. Be every patient; this is not an easy problem to correct.

If a child hesitates when pronouncing a word that begins with b or d, prompt him saying, "It's a b," or "It's a d." Quick reinforcement will help him overcome this problem. Saying words in lists gives greater problems than reading words in sentences—the sentence context helps.

Encouraging the Child

To successfully teach their child to read, parents must not only know how to teach him, but also must have enough patience, determination, and devotion to work day after day, usually for two or three years, helping him develop the skills he must acquire. They must never belittle their child when talking to their friends or tell him his brother or sister is smarter than he.

Teaching their child to read is not a now-and-then thing. If they neglect to hear him read for two or three days, his word recall suffers. They must love him enough to insist he read aloud to them daily and to constantly encourage him. Dyslexics, as well as other reading disabilities, include children who learn slowly, and children who are very bright. All need constant encouragement and one-to-one tutoring.

Tommy

In February, Tommy, a first grader, came to me to be tutored. Learning ordinary things was difficult for him. He was sure he could never learn to read; he knew only capital alphabet letters. He recognized only a few easy words. He did not know the sounds of the consonants and vowels. He was farsighted. I advised his parents to have his eyes tested. In less than three weeks he had glasses.

I tutored Tommy once weekly, planned his lessons carefully, and showed his mother how to tutor him. In April Tommy was finally ready to begin reading the first preprimer. Tommy continued to say, "I cannot learn to read. It is impossible." Of course, this interfered with his progress.

At the public library I found a book, *The Little Engine That Could*.[1] This book tells a story of a little blue train with a huge load of toys, which managed to chug up a mountain as it said, "I think I can, I think I can." When I read the story to Tommy, he enjoyed chanting, "I think I can, I think I can"—the chug-chug of the little engine. Tommy began to say, "I think I can, I think I can" when I asked him to read a page or spell a word. His self-image gradually improved. In time he began to say, "Don't help me with this phonics page. I can do it."

Tommy repeated the first grade, and his mother and I tutored him for several years. He did learn to read.

Dyslexia cannot be cured. The dyslexic has a different kind of mind. Often it is a gifted mind—many famous people have been dyslexics.

The dyslexic has no more problems than anyone else except those that come from being discouraged by his inability to learn words and recall them. Because of slow and incorrect word recall, he may find it impossible to learn to read in a regular classroom, and may need one-to-one instruction and carefully planned lessons.

Betty

Betty is a severe dyslexic. In the spring, after a year in first grade, her mother brought her to me to be tutored. Betty could not read; she recognized only six common words. I taught her the consonants by having her sort pictures into groups according to their initial sounds. Looking at pictures on a vowel chart helped her to learn the short vowels. Saying the sounds of letters as she traced their shapes on a rough masonite board helped her to recall them. I planned daily lessons for her and taught her mother how to tutor her. Word recall was very difficult for Betty. However, by the end of January she had finished reading three preprimers and knew 120 words.

"Am I retarded?" Betty asked me. "Is that the reason I am so slow at learning to read?"

---

1. Piper, Watty. *The Little Engine That Could*. New York: Platt & Munk Publishers, 1987.

"You are intelligent," I assured her. "You're not retarded. Many retarded children can read easy books. Because you are dyslexic, reading is difficult for you. If you keep at it and do your lessons with your mother faithfully, you will learn to read."

I tutored Betty once weekly for several years; her mother helped her with daily lessons. Betty learned to read and graduated from high school.

Teaching Words

There are two ways to teach a child to read words: by sight and by sounding them letter by letter. To teach the child to recognize a word by sight, show the child a printed word, tell him the word, and have him say it. Show him the word again and again, mixed in with a few words he already knows, until he recognizes it and says it immediately. Many English words are best taught by sight. Words such as know, said, eight, and light do not "sound out."

After the child has learned the letter sounds, he can begin to learn words by sounding them. Show the child a word and help him sound it out. Have him say it, then show him the word again and again until he recognizes it and can say it immediately without sounding it.

Some dyslexics learn words easier by sight than by sound, but the dyslexic will find learning to read difficult if he is taught vocabulary words only by sight. He may read the word home correctly in one paragraph and call it house in the next. Road may be street, and father, dad. It is very necessary for him to know phonics because his word recall is slow and inaccurate. He needs to know how to use phonics for unlocking the pronunciations of new words as well as for recalling words that he has forgotten.

A new word usually has to be reviewed once each day for three to five days to enable the child to make it a part of his reading vocabulary, but even then, if the word does not soon reoccur in his reading, he will forget it. By using phonics and context clues, he will be able to recall it.

Jay

Nine-year-old Jay could not read. His parents decided to enroll him in a school where he would be tutored one-to-one every day. All that school year Jay sounded lists of words.

In June, Jay came to me to be tutored. He had read three preprimers, could sound three-letter, short vowel words, and knew about thirty easy sight words. Of course, he was discouraged. He had sounded so many lists of words that he had formed the habit of "sounding out" words; he had not learned to recognize them by sight. When asked to read sentences, he continually stopped to "sound out" words, even those he knew well.

By playing an easy word game with him, I ascertained that he could learn words by sight. I showed his mother how to help him and assigned two groups of five reading vocabulary words to be learned by sight that week. Each day he was also to read and reread three pages aloud from a preprimer.

After sounding new words, Jay was taught to make them sight words. That summer Jay developed a reading vocabulary. He read three preprimers and more than 100 pages from a primer. Nevertheless, while he was reading, he had to be frequently reminded not to stop and sound words he already knew.

When you are teaching the child to read, you must continually observe his progress and push him forward. As soon as the beginner has learned two or three vowel sounds and some consonants, print easy three-letter words on small strips of paper so he can play games with you, maneuvering the words into sentences and reading them.

Reading is not just saying words. It is reading words in sentences and comprehending their meaning. The child will make very slow progress if most of the lesson time is spent on phonics and oral reading is neglected. He may begin to look critically at words he already knows, hesitating here and there to make sure he is saying them correctly. His reading will lose its fluency and his comprehension will suffer.

At least half of tutoring time should be spent on reading sentences, paragraphs, or stories. Each day the child should read and reread two or three pages from a basic reader. To develop his comprehension, he should talk about what he has just read.

Very Common Words and Phonics

There are 220 common English words that all children should be taught to recognize quickly because they are used in books again and again. The educator Edward W. Dolch spent seven years in the 1930s compiling this list after discovering that teaching children very common words as sight words made it easier to teach them to read. Flash cards containing these words—the Dolch Popper Words—and games based on them are widely used in the first, second, and third grades.

In Part Three of this book, there is a list, titled "Much Used Words," made up of Dolch's 220 words and 30 additional frequently used words. Because these words are used so often the child should learn to spell them. Knowing how will make it easier for him to write sentences and stories.

The dyslexic will find learning to read more difficult if he is taught only by the sight-word method. He needs phonetic skills to recall words, to unlock new ones, and to divide words into syllables.

Phonics should be taught in a useful, logical order—consonants, short vowels, long vowels, consonant digraphs, diphthongs, hard and soft c and g, and r-controlled vowels. As the child masters these skills, he should also be taught syllabication.

To be able to teach the child phonics, a parent must have a knowledge of phonics. How to teach phonics and syllabication is discussed at length in Part Two of this book.

If you learned to read mainly by memorizing sight words, you may have only a meager knowledge of phonics. You must be certain to say each letter's sound correctly when you introduce it to the child. If you say it part of the time incorrectly, the child will become confused.

Short vowel sounds are frequently mispronounced. Notice the initial short vowel sounds in the following lists of words:

Short a—act, add, animal, apple, ash, ax
Short e—ebb, edge, elephant, empty, end, ever
Short i—igloo, ill, image, inch, Indian, itch
Short o—object, octopus, odd, olive, opposite, ox
Short u—ugly, umbrella, umpire, unbend, under, upset

The child may find short vowel sounds very confusing. The short a, e, and i may seem to sound the same to him. Looking in a mirror at how wide his mouth is open and where his tongue is placed may be helpful. Making new words by changing the short vowels in three-letter words and asking him to pronounce them will help him overcome this problem. Examples: pan, pen, pin; bat, bet, bit; tan, ten, tin; ham, hem, him; bag, beg, big; pat, pet, pit.

Each dyslexic child is unique. He should have one-to-one instruction paced to fit his needs, for he may grasp one phonetic skill quickly and have difficulty with another.

The parent must remember to always encourage him. It may be necessary to review a skill many times before he masters it. Do not let this upset you. Be patient, brag about every bit of progress he makes. Never downgrade him when talking to your friends and discuss his problems with your spouse in private. If the child's parents are not supportive, he usually makes slower progress. To succeed he must feel that he *can* succeed.

Ned

Ned was very discouraged when he first came to be tutored. It was June; he had spent two years in the first grade. He had learned about fifty easy sight words and could read two short preprimers, but he had not mastered the consonant and vowel sounds. Because he had been unable to learn to read, he had been placed in the "special ed" class, except in math. He was good at math.

I tutored Ned one hour each week and planned a half-hour's daily homework for him. I made sure his mother sounded vowels correctly (she needed help in this area) and taught her how to tutor him.

At first Ned's progress was very slow. He frequently yawned; he was listless and sure that learning to read was almost impossible. However, as his reading skills began to improve, he became more attentive. With daily phonics and sight vocabulary drills, Ned's ability to recall words improved. He read and reread two pages from a basic reader series every day, stopping after each page to talk about what he'd just read. Soon he began completing his lessons at school. His "special ed" teacher continually praised and encouraged him.

Ned had a notebook in which we wrote phonics principles, followed by word examples of their sounds. When he was unsure of a sound, I would suggest he look it up in his notebook. He kept this with him for review.

At the third-grade reading level we began studying syllable rules. Soon Ned was able to divide words into syllables and pronounce them. His difficulty with word recall lessened, and his oral reading improved.

It was necessary for Ned to continue oral reading through the third grade. However, as his reading improved, I began to assign two pages to be read orally each day and one page to be read silently. He was asked to stop after each page and talk about what he had just read. He was also encouraged to tell stories in sequence—what happened first, next, and last.

Ned did not have to repeat any other grade in school. Recently, his mother told me that he is doing well in fifth grade. Ned says he plans to go to college on a soccer scholarship. He excels in soccer—he just might do it.

Talking With the Teacher

Parents may not realize their child is reading below grade level. Many report cards only inform them how well the child is reading in the basic reader being used in his reading group.

Suppose the child is in the last half of the fourth grade. He listens to the teacher's instructions and does his workbook lessons fairly well, but he is reading from a third-grade basic reader. His report card says, "Reading level first half of third grade. B." Of course, B means above average. The child's reading grade is reported in this manner to avoid discouraging him.

If his parents note only the B grade, they may feel their child is doing very well. They will not realize he has a reading disability until the teacher calls them in for a conference. If your child is reading below his grade level, do not despair. Do not, however, believe that given time he will catch up. Usually the child will not read for pleasure when reading is difficult; he will do only the reading required at school. As the books become more difficult, he will fall farther and farther behind.

Because your child is reading more than a year below grade level, you know that he needs help. Do not feel that he must be labeled dyslexic and placed in a "special ed" group. Instead, talk to his teacher. Assure her that you will help him at home, then begin to tutor him at once.

First, you must locate a reader of the right level. Perhaps the school will have one they will lend you. If they don't, ask the librarian at the public library for reading textbooks written at the child's level. Do not get the same book he is reading at school.

Choose a basic reader you feel the child will enjoy, and ask him to read two or three pages from the second story in the book. If he seems not to know a word, count five to yourself, then say it for him. Without his realizing it, keep count of the words he misses—do not include proper nouns. Let him roam the library while you count the number of words on the pages he just read. If he has missed more than five words out of one hundred, the book is too difficult to use for tutoring him. Select an easier book; a basic reader of that series one-half grade below might be a good choice. Reading textbooks of the same grade level vary in difficulty.

When a child tries to read a book that is too difficult, he becomes frustrated and makes little progress. He will do better reading orally from a book that is too easy than one that is too hard. Oral reading gives practice in word recall. Being able to recall common words without effort gives the child confidence and makes it easier for him to learn less familiar words.

It does not take hours of daily tutoring to bring the child's reading skills up to grade level. To learn to read a child must read orally. If he is guided properly and really tries, a half hour of daily one-to-one tutoring works wonders.

Belinda

In August, Belinda told her parents she definitely could not go to school that fall—they'd have to teach her at home. She cried as she told them all the children would laugh at her when she tried to read. She said, "Cursive writing is hard, and spelling twenty fourth-grade words is impossible."

In the third grade Belinda had tried to keep up with her classmates. Her teacher had been kind and thoughtful, but Belinda had found school very difficult. She was sure she could not succeed in fourth grade. Her parents brought her to me to be tutored.

I gave Belinda a few informal tests. In the English language there are 220 most-used words. Belinda knew almost all of these but very little phonics. She made letters backward—she couldn't tell the difference between p and g, and d and b.

As I talked with Belinda, I realized she is very intelligent. Because she is a dyslexic, she had found it impossible to learn to read well in the regular classroom. I handed her a one-inch strip of heavy paper and asked her to place it under the line she was reading and slide it down the page as she read orally from a second-grade reader. Belinda knew most of the words, but she did not read them in the order they were written. Words from the end of a sentence were mixed with those in its middle. It was easy to see why her classmates laughed at her reading.

I gave Belinda the reader used in the first half of the second grade and asked her to read three pages aloud to her mother each day, using the paper strip beneath each line, sliding it down the page as she read. Then I showed her mother how to guide Belinda's eye movements by pointing with a pencil to the words she was to read, moving it quickly above each line. When Belinda finished a page, they were to stop and talk about the story.

Belinda's parents asked for a conference with her fourth-grade teacher, and explained their daughter's problems. It was decided that Belinda was to be assigned only ten spelling words each week. She was to take her social studies and science books home so her parents could help her read the lessons. She was not granted the privilege of going to a resource teacher for help, they felt that she would eventually catch up.

Belinda enjoyed reading aloud to her mother. As she learned phonics skills, her spelling and word recall improved. By early spring she was able to master the weekly twenty-word spelling lesson, was doing satisfactory fourth-grade work, and was enjoying classroom activities.

During summer vacation Belinda stopped reading orally for a few weeks, and her reading began to lose its fluency. It will probably be necessary for her to continue reading aloud with her mother's guidance, at least twice a week, for some time. She should remember to use the one-inch paper strip, sliding it down the page beneath the lines as she reads. This should eventually improve her eye movements so that she will be able to keep her place and read fluently.

Psychometrist's Tests

The psychometrist administers psychological tests. These measure IQ's, behavior development, and motor development, and also test reading, language, and math skills to determine why a child is having difficulty in one or more of these areas.

A teacher may recommend that a child be tested by a psychometrist. These tests are helpful if the results are studied and the child is given special help in his weak areas. Parents should not be perturbed if the test scores are low. This may be because the child has had no previous experience in manipulating the type of materials used. His shyness may also have kept him from answering questions. He may be a child that is maturing very slowly—a child "young for his age."

Danny

When Danny was five years old, his speech was still difficult to understand. His mother, Kathy Carlston, took him to be tested by a psychometrist who told her the tests indicated that Danny was a "slow learner." He advised her to send Danny to preschool that fall and to kindergarten when he was six.

Kathy was quite upset. When she asked me to tutor Danny, I promised I would begin tutoring him after his preschool year. Meanwhile, there were things she should do to help him overcome his language disability— take him on trips to shopping malls, the children's museum, and the public library. On these trips she was to encourage him to talk about the things he saw. At the library they were to select picture books with short paragraphs on each page. As she read books to him, she was to stop often and encourage him to comment on the pictures.

Kathy was a very busy mother. She had two other lively boys, but she made time to read to Danny and provided experiences for him to talk about.

In June six-year-old Danny came to me for his first weekly lesson. He knew "The Alphabet Song" and could recognize most of the upper-case letters. He could count to thirteen. When I asked him to copy the letter a, he made it backward. I gave his mother a kindergarten workbook and asked her to teach him the sounds and shapes of two lower-case consonants that week. She was also to guide his hand as he practiced writing the letter a.

That summer I saw Danny nine times. I encouraged him to talk to me as he put easy puzzles together, made people from "people parts," arranged in sequence nursery rhyme pictures, and sorted small pictures of objects into groups with the same initial sounds. We sang a song about short vowels, and he counted pennies. September came. I hoped he would do well in kindergarten. In October, as Danny came through my door, he said, "I have a new spooky book my mother bought for me. Can I read it to you?"

"Oh, yes," I answered.

The book was twenty-six pages long, and its paragraphs were illustrated with pictures. Danny turned the pages one by one, talking about each picture, using phrases written beside it. Of course, he was repeating the phrases from memory—his mother had read the book to him three times. I knew then that this child would not continue to be a slow learner—he was just slow in maturing.

Danny is a dyslexic. It was difficult for him to recall reading vocabulary words and words he wanted to use in conversations. His mother and I worked with him patiently for three years. He was blessed with a curious mind.

When he was in the first and second grades, in the middle of his lessons I stopped for "encyclopedia breaks." As Danny entered my door, he told me the topic he wanted to look up that day. These varied: dinosaurs, sharks, the solar system, the Milky Way, the black hole, Bigfoot, the Alamo, the Titanic, opossums—the list went on and on. After Danny had located a topic in an encyclopedia, he read about it aloud as I supplied the words he did not know.

Of course he learned to read. How else could he satisfy his curiosity? He is now in the sixth grade and is a "Volunteer Mysteries in History" guide at the children's museum.

The Older Child

I feel quite certain that every person of average or above average intelligence can learn to read. The tutor, however, must come up with a way to reach a child, assuring him that he can learn to read and encouraging him to keep at it until he succeeds.

Joe

When I was searching for a seamstress to alter a dress, I met Joe Edwards's mother. She was concerned because her son was having difficulty learning to read.

"Joe is in the fifth grade," she said. "He learns many things easily. Although he cannot read the textbooks, he does well in the social studies and science class discussions. He's being sent to the remedial reading room part of each day." She asked me to tutor him.

Joe came to me in November. He was a handsome boy, almost eleven years old. He could not read first-grade material fluently, had little knowledge of consonant and vowel sounds, and confused b's and d's. He read to me slowly from a second-grade reader, saying some words correctly and fitting in others that he thought might be appropriate.

To test Joe's listening ability, I read a fifth-grade factual paragraph to him. He repeated it back to me almost verbatim. It was easy to see that he had excellent listening skills and was very intelligent.

At what reading level should I begin Joe's instruction?" I pondered. "The last part of the first grade would be the best level, but if I hand him a first-grade reader he will be insulted. The first second-grade reader would be better, but he probably knows only about ninety percent of its words. He may stumble over many of them and become frustrated. His memory seems to be very good—I'll try a different approach."

I handed him a one-inch strip of heavy paper and asked him to slide it down the page of the reader as I slowly read the page to him. Then I asked him to read the same page as I slid the strip slowly down it. He read it to me, supplying from memory the words that were not in his reading vocabulary. To help him learn these new words, I asked him to reread the page. After reading two pages together, we stopped and talked about the characters in the story.

Then we began our study of phonics by composing three-letter words using the short vowel a. I gave Joe a sheet of these words to say to his mother daily.

When Mrs. Edwards came to pick up her son, I showed her how I had helped Joe read from the second grade reader and asked her to tutor Joe using the same procedure. He was to read and reread two pages each day.

After a couple months of heavy phonics training and drill on reading vocabulary words, Joe said to me, "You don't need to read a page first for me anymore. I can read it." And he could. Then I changed his daily reading to this procedure:

1. Joe reads a page.
2. Joe's mother reads the same page.
3. Joe rereads the page.
4. They talk about it. Joe may be asked to tell in detail or in two or three sentences what has just happened in the story, and Joe's mother may ask, "What do you think will happen next?"

Joe's memory aided him in learning facts. For word recall he needed phonics and syllabication. We played many games that taught phonics sounds; syllable games became his favorites. Mrs. Edwards and I tutored Joe for three-and-a-half years. At the end of each school year he was promoted to the next grade. He learned to read and did well in high school.

The method I used for increasing Joe's reading vocabulary would not work with most children. Tutors and parents must vary their approach to fit the child, and the basic reader selected should be easy enough for the child to read without becoming frustrated. If he already knows ninety-five out of one hundred words, he will find it possible to learn and recall the five that are new to him. This will increase his confidence and make it easier for him to succeed.

Choral reading (reading aloud together) is very helpful to the child whose reading is two or more years below grade level. Go to the library and ask the librarian to help you select a high-interest book at the child's present reading level. Read three or four pages together, letting the child's voice take the lead until you see an unfamiliar word coming up, then you should take the lead long enough to pronounce it. Stop now and then to remark about something in the story. This is an excellent way to improve the child's word recall and enlarge his vocabulary.

Comprehension

A child may memorize many words, say them correctly, and get no thought from them. He is saying words, not reading. Reading is getting the thought the printed sentences were meant to convey.

At first the young child must read orally to get meaning from words grouped into sentences. He looks at one word at a time and says it; when he finishes a page he may not know what he just read. His mother should read the page for him, grouping the words together so they convey their intended meaning. Then she should ask him to reread the page, saying, "Make it sound like you are talking."

The child with a reading disability needs to continue reading and rereading pages orally throughout the first, second, and sometimes part of the third grade. If he has trouble learning to phrase, slide your pencil point quickly above the line of words, pointing to the end of each phrase. Example:

The little boy ran around the bear cage into the center of the zoo. He saw a pool with sea lions in it. He watched the seals swim and catch fish in the air.

Stop at the end of the paragraph and ask him to tell you what he has just read. As he reads the pages, stop often to talk about something of interest in the story. This will increase his ability to get thought from the words he is reading.

Jimmy

It was the first week of school. The fourth graders were reading orally from their new readers. Jimmy, a mischievous-looking boy in the back row, stood up and began to read slowly, word-for-word. At first I thought he was putting on an act, then I realized he was totally concerned with saying the words correctly. But he was getting no meaning from the sentences in the paragraph he was reading.

I set time aside to work with Jimmy alone, fifteen minutes, three times weekly. As he read to me orally from the basic reader, I quickly moved my pencil above the line of words, stopping briefly where phrases ended. Now and then I read a paragraph to him, emphasizing the phrasing. We stopped frequently to talk about what he had read.

Jimmy's reading slowly improved, and common words became more familiar. As he learned to combine words into phrases and sentences, he began to read smoothly and to get the thought from the printed symbols.

It is very important to talk about the stories and articles the child is reading, for he may seem to be reading very well when he reads a paragraph orally. His phrasing and expressions may be good, yet he may be getting very little thought from the words he is saying. His parents may not awaken to the fact that he has a reading disability until he fails social studies, science, or math tests. They are sure he read each of the lessons assigned, why couldn't he find the correct answers to the questions? Also, if he's so good at math, why does he get wrong answers to the story problems?

Kevin

Kevin came to me in June. His mother felt that he should be tutored before he entered seventh grade. Although his oral reading sounded excellent, his mother noticed that he got very little thought from the pages he read.

My tests showed that Kevin's comprehension level was the beginning of fourth grade. His word recall was good—he was not a dyslexic. He did not need phonics and syllabication. He had apparently formed the habit of saying words without attaching meaning to them—somewhat the same as you might do, when, after supposedly reading a page, you begin reading the next and suddenly realize you have no idea what the previous page was about.

To correct Kevin's problem, it was necessary to begin his lessons at his true comprehension level. Because I wanted him to succeed comfortably, we worked for three weeks at the third-grade level and then went on to the fourth grade. I taught him to use clue words to locate answers and to find the main ideas in paragraphs. He was to read silently when doing most of his homework and several pages orally each day to his mother, stopping now and then to talk with her about what he'd just read.

During that summer Kevin's reading comprehension improved. However, to correct this problem takes time and perseverance. The child whose parents have always talked with him about the stories and articles he is reading is indeed fortunate.

If your child's comprehension is weak:

1. Select an interesting story at a level he is able to comprehend, making sure ninety-eight percent of the words are in his reading vocabulary. Ask him to read a page aloud and tell you what he read. Encourage him to tell the happenings in proper sequence.
2. If he is unable to do this, have him reread the page silently, stopping after each paragraph to tell you that part of the story.
3. As his comprehension improves, increase the number of paragraphs he reads aloud until he is able to read an entire page and then tell the story in sequence.
4. As soon as he is able to comprehend the meaning of an entire page that he has read orally, he should be asked to read a page silently and tell you what he just read.
5. If he cannot tell the story in sequence, have him read one paragraph at a time silently and tell that part of the story. Continue this exercise until he is able to tell the events from an entire page in sequence.
6. To help build his comprehension, stop now and then to ask questions such as: What do you think will happen next? How do you think the story will end?

I have frequently advised parents to use this procedure, and they have found it an excellent way to develop their child's comprehension.

Spelling

Spelling is easy for some children, difficult for others. I have often been amazed at how quickly a person's spelling improves once he has learned the basic principles of phonics and syllabication.

Meg

Meg, a bright high school sophomore, found spelling difficult. When writing an assignment, she asked her mother how to spell many words. Her knowledge of phonics was vague.

In November I began tutoring her in reading and spelling. For about one half hour each week we worked on phonics, syllabication, and spelling, and every week I handed her a list of about thirty reading vocabulary words—fourth-, fifth-, and sixth-grade levels—to divide into syllables. After she divided them, I had her pronounce each word as we checked to see if the divisions were okay, and we talked about the phonetic principles involved as we corrected the syllabications. Then I pronounced each word, she wrote it down, and I spelled it back to her in syllables. She listed the misspelled words in her notebook.

At the end of three months Meg was able to spell eighty-five to ninety percent of a list of words. She had not studied them as a spelling lesson; she was able to write them correctly because she had learned the common rules for dividing words into syllables and knew the basic phonics rules that are used in sounding words.

After six months Meg missed only one or two words in a thirty-word list; often she spelled an entire list correctly.

Asking the child to memorize many spelling rules seems to be of little help. Teaching a child to write each syllable as he sounds it makes spelling much easier.

Recently a mother asked me, "Why don't my children remember their spelling words? They know them when they take their tests, but by the next weekend they've forgotten them."

A child will soon forget how to spell words if he does not use them in writing sentences. After the child has practiced writing the week's spelling lesson, make up one or two sentences composed of common words he has learned, saying each word slowly as he writes it. Encourage him to write short notes, friendly letters, and stories. Using common words frequently in his writing will help him remember how to spell them.

Written Work

The dyslexic may actually know the answers in a test, but be unable to read the questions and spell the words needed in the answers fast enough to complete them. If your child has a severe reading disability, check to see if his school has a resource teacher who can give him tests orally or can help him with reading and spelling.

The child, with the parent's help, should correct all written work. If he doesn't correct his errors, he ends up knowing little more than he knew before he did the assignment. His teacher grades his papers, then passes them back to him. The child usually glances at his paper. If the grade is an A, he takes it home to show to his parents. If it is an F, unless his parents insist on seeing all his written work, he tosses it in the wastebasket. This test has only provided his teacher with a grade for his or her records. The F may have made the child feel that trying to learn that subject is impossible.

If, however, the child's parents insist on seeing all his written papers, they can help him correct his errors. They can encourage him, note his efforts to improve, and praise his progress.

In some classrooms each child corrects his own written lessons with a red pencil, thus turning test-taking into a learning experience. The teacher collects the papers, records the grades, and passes the papers back. When the child brings them home, the parent should go over the tests with him to help him remember the correct answers to the items missed.

Encourage the child to write short notes, friendly letters, and stories. If he asks how to spell a word, tell him. Asking him to look up its spelling might cause him to forget what he was going to write.

Story writing is a creative process. Do not hinder his development by suggesting he change his wording. The child should be encouraged to develop his own way of expressing his thoughts, his own unique style.

Never dishearten him by correcting too many errors at one time—he might think you are finding fault with his story. Introduce the rules of punctuation gradually, one or two at a time. Teach the child to proofread his stories, reading them aloud to himself alone, correcting punctuation, and looking up the spelling of the words he is not sure of. When he's finished his story, have him read it to you. Praise it and correct only a few errors.

Hannah

Hannah is a dyslexic. I had tutored her for only a few months. She had finished reading a primer and was reading a first-grade reader when she wrote this, her first story.

> The Sad blue
> there war crans all the collrs
> war yousd But blue.
> No one liked blue.
> Butone gile liked blue.
>   The end   Hannah

She read it to me: "The Sad Blue. There were crayons. All the colors were used but blue. No one liked blue, but one girl liked blue. The end."

Hannah's story was good; it showed originality. She had put her thoughts into sentences and spelled words by sounding them.

"I really like your story," I told her. Then I read it aloud. "Your sentences are good, and you sounded out the spelling of the words quite well. The word were is spelled w-e-r-e. You can't tell this by sounding it. That's the reason you have to study spelling. Used is a word. Just write the letter u for its long sound. How would you spell it?"

"U-s-d," Hannah answered.

"Used has two vowels. It has an e in it," I said. "Where do you think the e should be?"

Of course Hannah put the e before the d because she knew that ed is a word ending.

"Every word has a vowel in it. Where would you put the vowel i in the word girl?"

"Before the r," Hannah said, "g-i-r-l."

"Right," I said, then again I praised Hannah's story. I did not mention the other errors. If a tutor corrects too many errors, the child will become discouraged and cease trying to put his thoughts into written words.

A third-grade teacher told me this story: After spending several weeks teaching her pupils punctuation and capitalization, she asked them to write stories. She took them home, corrected all the errors, and passed them back to the authors.

After two little boys had looked at their corrected stories, they came up to her desk, hand in hand. "Mrs. S," they said, "We will NEVER write you another story."

Developing a Reading Vocabulary

A person is never too old to learn to read, but it is often difficult for the older child or for an adult to get the daily one-to-one help needed to develop a reading vocabulary and reading comprehension.

Matt

One January day more than a dozen years ago, Linda Smith phoned me to ask if I would teach Matt, her husband, to read. I made an appointment to talk with him the following Saturday.

Matt arrived on time. He was twenty-four years old, tall, and good-looking. He told me that he had graduated from high school even though he had been unable to learn to read; His mother had read his lessons to him and helped him with the written work. Now he had steady employment in the shipping department of a large company. He liked it, but he could not hope for promotions because he could not read instructions. He needed to increase his earnings; he had two young sons, and would like to be able to read to them.

When Matt was in elementary school, his parents had had him tutored. Unfortunately, the tutor did not know how to teach a dyslexic to read. Matt had copied many pages from books, but that hadn't helped him in reading. His handwriting was smooth and legible.

The informal tests I gave Matt showed that he read orally at mid-second-grade level and silently at beginning third grade. He seemed to know most of Dolch's list of common words but frequently had difficulty in recalling them. He did not know the vowel sounds and could not sound words.

Matt came for lessons one hour each week for several years. He filled blanks in phonics workbooks, pronounced word lists from the *Victory Drill Book*[1], and learned to sound out words. For a short time he read orally to his wife but soon found this upsetting. I taped cassettes of the *Victory Drill Books'* word lists, instructing him to read the words one at a time, pausing after each one to check its pronunciation with the voice on the cassette. I also taped stories from basic readers for him to read along with. Gradually, Matt's reading improved; he read the third, fourth, fifth, and part of the sixth-grade readers.[2]

I asked Matt to keep a record of how much time he spent reading during the week. Matt read during his breaks at work—often four, five, and even six hours. Once in a while his total was less than three hours.

When he was finally able to read newspapers, sports magazines, *Readers Digest*, *Time*, and car manuals, I suggested he stop coming for lessons. He told me he had noticed that when he neglected reading for a few days his ability to recall words fell rapidly. He didn't want to discontinue his lessons; he felt the encouragement he received kept him from neglecting daily reading. Soon after this, Matt moved away, and I lost touch with him.

Dyslexics have difficulty recalling words. As soon as the child has learned enough common words to read preprimers, if he continues reading very easy books every day, he is usually able to recall the words he has learned and gradually build up a reading vocabulary. If he reads only now and then, he forgets the words, begins substituting others, becomes discouraged, and makes little progress.

Easygoing love may lead a parent to neglect daily reading. There are so many things that make it difficult to read daily—the child wants to play; he is tired; he has homework. There are phone calls, visiting relatives, birthday parties, and grocery shopping. The list goes on and on. If the child's reading is often neglected, he assumes it is unimportant and ceases to cooperate.

To teach their child to read, parents need proper materials and know-how, but most of all they must have tough love—love strong enough to

---

1. Enderlin, August C. *Victory Drill Book.*
2. Matt's need for adult reading comprehension workbooks led me to write *The Curious Readers*, a seven book series, SRA, published by McGraw-Hill.

enable them to find the time every day, to help their child to make continuous progress. Reading must be a part of the child's daily routine—the same as getting up in the morning, attending school, eating meals, and going to bed at night. The child's parents must be enthusiastic and supportive. Daily practice brings success.

Games

Games, properly selected, are learning tools that can be used to strengthen the child's phonetic and syllabication skills and increase his reading vocabulary. School supply stores stock a wide variety of games—phonics and syllable-card games, game boards to use when teaching blends, and a variety of bingo games. There are also games the child can play alone—puzzles, mazes, and self-checking card games.

Assembling puzzles develops skill in spatial analysis. The puzzles selected should not be too difficult and should be put together on a movable board so the child can work on them at odd times. Parents can keep the child from becoming bored and discouraged by now and then directing his attention to the shape, size, or color on the edge of one of the puzzle's pieces.

Solving mazes develops critical thinking and cognitive skills. Matching a word to a picture and then checking the answer by looking at the back of the card increases the child's reading vocabulary.

Games cannot take the place of daily oral reading or vocabulary drill. At home the dyslexic can play games in the evening and invite his friends to join in the fun. Playing games together develops a feeling of empathy. A tutor should reserve ten to fifteen minutes at the end of the child's one-hour lesson for a game that strengthens a weak area. If the child usually wins (and the tutor is adept at losing), he will go home with a feeling of accomplishment.

The busy tutor seldom has the time and materials to create games, but he or she can easily change games purchased at the school supply store into ones that will review and strengthen the skills being taught. Adding pictures of objects that begin with blends will increase the use of blend gameboards. Typing and color-coding vocabulary cards will provide games usable at different reading levels. Easy-word playing cards can be used to create short and long vowel games.

One of my favorite games is a bingo game that features the 220 most-used English words. I've changed the rules for play; instead of clearing the cards when a person says, "Bingo," I hand him a token and continue playing until all the words have been called. The winner is the person who has the most tokens.

By appointing the child as caller and handing him word cards to be used when calling, I can put aside the words he does not know and at the end of the game ask him to learn them.

Tony

Tony, a second grader, was reading word-for-word and needed practice in phrasing. I separated sight-phrase cards into three stacks: phrases that could be used as subjects, those that could be used as predicates, and phrase modifiers. I placed the three stacks face down on the table and turned up four cards in front of each stack. Then Tony and I took turns making sentences, adding new cards as needed. He enjoyed this game and soon began to read its phrases.

Tony plays checkers at home—and is quite an expert. His favorite game is Vowel Checkers, a game played on a checkerboard imprinted with missing-vowel words. As he moves the checkers he says the needed vowels and words. Ten minutes after we begin playing, we are hopelessly deadlocked, and if I relax for a second, he wins.

Jon

A child may invent a game to ward off boredom. As long as the game is not too time consuming, I encourage this.

Jon, a fourth grader, marks all the answers on a multiple-choice worksheet before beginning the lesson, then reads it and selects the true answers. It pleases him if several of his "guesses" are correct. From experience he has learned that guessing will never get him an A.

Jon's favorite game is "Concentration in Classification," a complex one he and I created from sixteen four-card groups of syllable nouns and a game board. When we play, he wins—it's a good ego booster.

Part 2

How to Tutor
Your Child
One-to-One

How to Begin

English words are formed from the letters of the alphabet. The first step in teaching the child to read is teaching him to say the alphabet and recognize its letters.

There is a very old alphabet song chanted to the tune of "Twinkle, Twinkle, Little Star," which is sung in kindergarten and first grade, wherever English reading is taught. A friend tells me she learned this song in first grade more than sixty years ago. Her version is:

THE ALPHABET SONG

A, b, c, d, e, f, g,
H, i, j, k, l, m, n, o, p,
Q, r, s, and t, u, v,
W—x, y, and z.
Now I've said my ABC's,
Tell me what you think of me.

When I asked friends, young and old, if they had learned "The Alphabet Song" they chanted it, sometimes changing its last line.

Make up an ending you think the child will like and teach him to sing "The Alphabet Song." Sing the song around the house. You can make it fun by inventing different ending lines—but be sure the child learns to chant the letters in order.

Purchase a set of alphabet letters at the toy store. There are two kinds of sets, upper-case and lower-case. Upper-case letters are capitals; you need not purchase these, only the lower-case set.

Lay the lower-case letters on the table in front of the child and have him arrange them in alphabetical order as he sings "The Alphabet Song."

As soon as he has learned the names of the letters, begin teaching him the sounds of the vowels and consonants. The letters **a, e, i, o,** and **u** are vowels; the others are consonants. Spend the first part of each lesson on vowels, the balance on teaching consonant sounds.

Vowels

Teach the short vowel sounds first. These words all begin with short vowels: **a,** at; **e,** egg; **i,** in; **o,** ox; **u,** up. The long vowels have the same sound as their alphabet names: **a,** ate; **e,** eat; **i,** I'm; **o,** oat; **u,** unite.

There is a vowel song that young children like to chant; you and your child can make up the tune. Chant this song saying the short vowel sounds instead of the letter's name. Each short vowel has the sound of the vowel that begins the noun that follows it.

SHORT VOWEL SONG

A, a, a for apple,
E, e, e for egg,
I, i, i for Indian hopping on one leg,
O, o, o for ostrich living in the zoo,
U, u, u for umbrella to keep the rain off of you.
Now I've said my vowels,
A, e, i, o, u.
I hope you like this little song
That I sang for you.

Use a vowel chart when teaching the short and long vowel sounds. Teach your child to read it, saying the short vowel sound before saying the name of the picture, and the long vowel sound after the picture's name as shown on the vowel chart on the next page.

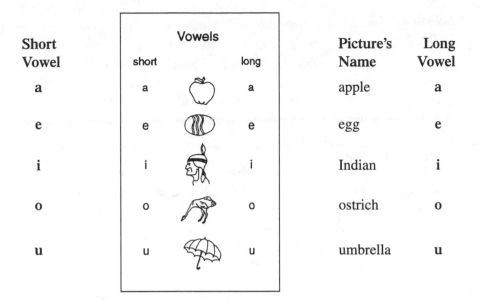

Short Vowel	Vowels		Picture's Name	Long Vowel
	short	long		
a	a	a	apple	a
e	e	e	egg	e
i	i	i	Indian	i
o	o	o	ostrich	o
u	u	u	umbrella	u

It is very important to repeat this vowel chart daily until the child is very sure of the short vowel sounds. (There are two vowel charts in Part Three of this book.)

A small mirror can help the child who is having difficulty hearing and saying short vowel sounds. Ask him to hold the mirror six inches from his face as he repeats the short vowels. Call his attention to how wide he opens his mouth, where his tongue is, and the shape his lips make as he says each sound.

Young children may find the following way of learning the short vowels helpful. Draw out the sound of each short vowel as you say it.

a   Place your hand out flat under your chin. Say, "a, apple," drawing the sound out.

e   Place your hands on both sides of your mouth, push back slightly, and say, "e, egg."

i   Put your thumb under your chin. Say, "i, ick, icky, i."

o   Say "o" with your head back, as if doctor is looking down your throat.

u   Say, "u, uh, underwear."

Consonants

If possible, set aside a half hour for the child's lesson each weekday, Monday through Saturday. The child with a reading disability makes better progress if he is taught every day. Choose a time when he is not overly tired, a period usually free from interruptions. Begin each lesson by having the child read the chart of short and long vowel sounds. Listen carefully to make certain he is saying each sound correctly. Then teach him the sound of a consonant.

Teach the sound of the letter f first. Print a large f on a strip of paper. Place the strip on the table before the child and say, "The letter f has the sound you hear at the beginning of the word feather. Say the sound with me—f, f, feather. Notice that when you make this sound your mouth is almost closed, and you blow air through your front teeth—f, feather." Have the child say the word several times, drawing out the sound of the consonant f.

Look for pictures of objects that begin with an f. Try to find at least five small pictures of objects such as a feather, foot, fence, fish, and fan. Put these in an envelope and save them.

Make a large, lower case f, four or five inches long, the large "cane" first. Guide your child's finger over the f, using the proper writing motion. Then have him say the sound as he traces the letter with his finger.

When he has learned to trace the letter easily, have him make its shape with his finger, first on the table, then on a chalkboard or large sheet of unlined paper.

A chalkboard is an excellent place on which to teach a child to write. Always write the letters very large—four or five inches tall. Never urge a child to write small; that may cause his writing to become cramped.

After he has learned to make the lower-case f, teach him to print the upper-case F. Say, "This is the capital letter F. If a person's name begins with f, use the capital F. Capital letters are always used at the beginning of names and the beginning of sentences."

Teach the consonants one at a time, making sure each sound is mastered before proceeding to the next.

The following chart lists the consonants with objects whose names begin with the consonant's sounds. Teach these in the order given below. Remember to save the pictures you collect, placing them in separate envelopes. There are pages of pictures for use in teaching initial consonants and a manuscript chart with lower-case and upper-case letters in Part Three of this book.

Consonant Chart

f	football, fence, feather, fan, foot, fish
t	turtle, table, tomato, truck, tent, toad
c	(the hard sound) corn, cat, comb, car, cake, coat
b	bird, bed, baby, barn, boat, bike
h	hand, horn, horse, hoe, house, hat
m	mail, map, mitten, mouse, mule, mountain
w	window, watch, witch, web, wagon, windmill
s	socks, shoes, sun, saw, sweater, seal
g	girl, goat, gun, gate, ghost, globe
d	duck, dog, doctor, drum, deer, doll
n	nest, nut, needle, nail, net, nurse
l	lion, leaf, lock, lamp, ladder, lighthouse
r	radio, rake, rope, rat, ring, rabbit
p	pretzel, pig, pie, parrot, pumpkin, policeman
k	kite, kettle, key, kitten, kangaroo, king
j	jar, jeep, jacket, jug, jet
v	volcano, valentine, vase, violin, violet
y	yoyo, yarn
z	zebra, zoo, zipper, zigzag, zero
qu	question mark, queen

The letter **u** always follows **q**. This **u** is silent, it does not have a vowel sound. Perhaps you will notice that the letter **x** is not included in the above chart. Introduce its sound when you have a word that begins with **ex**.

As soon as the child has learned four or five consonants, mix up the consonant pictures you have been saving in envelopes. Have the child sort them out and replace them in the envelopes. Make it a game; mix pictures from three or four envelopes together, place their initial letters on the table, and have the child say the names of the objects in the pictures as he places them in columns beneath their initial letters. When he has finished doing this, the consonant that has the most pictures wins the game. The child will be pleased when he succeeds in correctly sorting the pictures. Praise him—tell him he's doing really well at learning consonant sounds.

It is very important to pace your teaching to the child's learning speed. Remember, never be impatient or act rushed. For him, learning to read is difficult. Do not discourage him by being cross. Be pleased at his progress and boost his ego. The more sure of himself he feels, the faster he will learn.

Review the vowel sounds and two to four consonants each day. Do not add new consonants to be learned until he knows the sounds of those you have been teaching. However, do not proceed so slowly that he becomes bored.

Get out the lower-case letters and spell short words. Lay out the vowels in a line on one side. Tell him that every word must have a vowel sound. Say, "Can you put three letters together to make the word cat? Can you change it to the word bat? Bit? Fit? Fib? Can you spell fat? Cab? Bet?"

Sounding Short Vowel, Three-Letter Words

When all the consonants have been learned, the child is ready to begin sounding out three-letter, short vowel words. He is also ready to begin reading the first preprimer.

The following lists of words are to be used in teaching a child to sound short vowel words. They are not to be taught as sight words; the child is to learn them by sounding the letters. Put these words on flash cards and mix them up each time you have the child say them. Teach one group at a time in the following order:

a   cat, jam, tap, fan, wag, pan, gas, ham, mat, bag, lap, sack
i   dig, win, sip, pin, tip, did, Jim, zip, big, fin, him, wig
o   lot, dog, jog, pod, Tom, mop, job, not, nod, top, rot, fog
u   bug, fun, bus, rug, hum, tub, pup, gum, bud, sun, must, nut
e   red, hen, leg, net, yes, web, ten, egg, men, jet, beg, wet

(The short **e** words are listed last because many children find the short **e** the most difficult vowel to pronounce.)

Begin with the short a list. Have the child sound each letter—c, a, t— then say the word. If the child has difficulty synthesizing (combining) its sounds into a word, sound its letters for him several times, first slowly and then more and more quickly until he recognizes that the sounds are the word cat. Be patient. He will soon catch on and be pleased with his own progress.

As soon as the child has learned to sound one short vowel word list easily, teach him to sound the next word list. When he has mastered its words, mix the two lists together and have him sound these words, making sure he sounds the short vowels correctly. (There are short vowel lists in Part Three of this book.)

Sight Words

In the 1930s, Dr. Edward W. Dolch made a list of the 220 English words that are most used in reading and writing. These are included in the list titled "Most Used Words" in Part Three of this book. Make flash cards of these words and take the list to a quick-print shop. Show the printer the size of the print in a preprimer and have him photocopy them that size. Cut the words apart, attach each word to the center of a card with Scotch tape, and arrange the cards in order. Write the letter of its group on the back of each card.

When the child has mastered the sounds of eight or more consonants and the five short vowel sounds and can also "make" three-letter short vowel words, he is ready to begin learning this list of words. Grouping the words in the order given five at a time, teach them as sight words; do not ask the child to sound them.

Say each word as you lay its card on the table in front of the child and have him repeat the word after you. Mix the cards again. Lay them on the table. Say, "Pick up _____. Say the word as you lay it down."

Do this with five words that need to be reviewed and five new sight words. When the child has almost learned the words, ask him if he wants to be the "teacher," saying the word card that is to be picked up.

Make your word drill last long enough for the child to learn the words. The child should always pick up the cards and say the words on them at least three times during the drill, otherwise he may not be able to remember them.

Children enjoy playing this word game: Mix together eight or twelve word cards. Lay them face-up on the table in four columns, then say, "Let's have a race to see who can get the most words. Make an imaginary little man with your second and third fingers. Have him walk across the table to the word I say. Now let's both place our hands on the edge of the table. Are you ready to begin?" Say a word. Hesitate so the child's "little man" reaches the word first. Have him say it and place the card on his side of the table. Say the words he does not know and place them on your side of the table. When he has mastered most of the words, let him be the "teacher," arranging the words on the table and saying the word that is to be picked up. Of course, you must hesitate long enough for him to win most of the cards.

Never let a child guess at a sight word. If he guesses a word wrong, it will take him longer to learn it. If he hesitates, give him the length of time it takes you to count one, two, three slowly to yourself, then say the word for him.

Repeat each group of sight words each day until they can be said without hesitation. These words are not to be sounded; if the child hesitates trying to remember a word, say it for him.

As soon as one group of words is mastered, add another group. If all the words except one have been learned, make the next group using that word and four more. Stack the sight words that the child has learned together. Play games with them.

When the child has finished Group A of the Most Used Words, stack them together. Put a rubber band around them so that if a word is forgotten, it can be easily located and reviewed.

Discontinue weekly work on these words when you begin the preprimer vocabulary word lists. The preprimer's vocabulary words are sight words.

Save the sight-word cards. Review those already learned and use them in playing word games. You will need to teach the balance of them in the first and second grades.

You can purchase Dolch's 220 sight-word flash cards, the DOLCH POPPER WORDS, Sets 1 and 2, and an excellent bingo game, the DOLCH GROUP WORD TEACHING GAME.[1]

If you decide to use the Popper Words, you need not make flash cards of the Most Used Words. Instead, arrange the Popper Words alphabetically, then group them in somewhat the same order as in the Most Used Words lists. Save the lists for spelling lessons.

Playing the Dolch Group Word Teaching Game is a good way to review the 220 most used English words. If you appoint the child caller, hand out tokens when a person bingos, and end the game when all the words have been called. You can put aside the words the child did not know and ask him to learn them.

---

1. The Dolch product copyright has been sold again and again since Edward W. Dolch's death in 1961. At present, McGraw Hill publishes the Dolch products. They can be ordered from the following address: SRA, P.O. Box 543, Blacklick, OH 43004; (800) 843-8855.

The Preprimers

Preprimer Reading Readiness

The child is ready to read his first preprimer if:

1. He recognizes the letters of the alphabet and knows the sounds of the consonants and short vowels.
2. He can put letters together to spell common three-letter, short vowel words.
3. He knows that words in sentences are read from left to right.
4. He knows the vocabulary words used on the first fifteen pages of the first preprimer.

Selecting Reading Books

Soon after you decide to teach your child, you should start looking for the basic reading books to use. It may take several weeks to find them. When the child has learned the sounds of most of the consonants and short vowels, you must have all of the first-grade readers so you can begin teaching him the preprimer vocabulary words.

The best preprimers have very easy short sentences and an easy-to-learn vocabulary. They have many pictures, and their stories are of interest to young children. The public school in your area has preprimers, and the public libraries have them in their easy-to-read section. The vocabularies in the books you use should build up gradually through the first, second, and third preprimers, the primer, the first-grade reader, and the two second-grade books. For this reason, if possible, select books that are part of the same reading series.

In the back of each of these textbooks there should be a word list of all the new words used on each page. Do not select books that have no word lists unless you have access to the lists in their teacher's manuals. Books with easy, familiar words are better than those with uncommon and difficult words and names.

The Macmillan Company, Holt, Rinehart and Winston, Houghton Mifflin Company, and Scott, Foresman and Company have published very good reading textbooks.[1] Some excellent reading books were published in the 1970s. Many of those published prior to the 1970s lack interest. I would not use these. Ask a public or private school in your area for help in securing the textbooks you need. Do not use the same books the child is reading at school.

Teaching the Preprimer

Before you hand the child his first preprimer, teach him all the words he should know in order to read its first fifteen pages. This will probably be about fifteen words.

I find taking a reading book to a quick-print shop a great time-saver. Show the printer the size of the words on the preprimer pages the child is to read and ask him to photocopy the words on the word list, enlarging them to that size. If possible, have the lists of the three preprimers photocopied then. These lists are short; you will save time by preparing the word cards for all three preprimers at one time.

Cut the words apart. Attach each word to the center of a card with Scotch tape, and on its back write the number of the preprimer's page on which that word was first used.

After you have attached each book's words to cards, put a rubber band around each group, then press the stack of cards together tightly, and color one edge with a marking pencil. Use a different color for each book. Later, if the groups get mixed together, you can easily rearrange them.

Teach these vocabulary words as sight words, five at a time. When the

---

1. I use The Macmillan Reading Program (1974) for grades one, two, and three. The stories are interesting and its vocabulary builds up gradually without difficult proper names. I also use Series R Macmillan Reading Books (1983) for grades one through six. These are published by the Macmillan Publishing Company.

child has learned all the words on the first fifteen pages of the first preprimer, he is ready to start reading it.

Praise him. Let him know that he has done well. Hand him the first preprimer. Give him time to look at the pictures and talk about them. He will be delighted to discover that he can read page after page of his new book. There are just a few words on the beginning pages of a preprimer. After he reads a page aloud, you should read it slowly, saying the sentences with enthusiasm and meaning.

As soon as the preprimer's pages begin to have more than three lines of words, follow this procedure:

1. Cut a strip of heavy paper one inch wide and nine inches long. Lay this on the preprimer's page under the first line of words that the child is to read. As the child reads each page aloud, slide the paper strip down, line by line. The strip will help him keep his place on the page and train his eyes to move from left to right as he reads.

2. If a child hesitates because he cannot recall a word, wait as long as it takes you to count one, two, three slowly, then say the word for him. Do not give him time to guess it. Never ask him to sound it. Reading vocabulary words are sight words. Prompting the child will keep him from being upset and losing his train of thought.

3. As soon as the child has finished reading a page, ask him to slide the paper strip down the page, line by line, as you read it slowly with meaning.

4. Have the child reread the page aloud, sliding the strip down the page as he reads.

5. Talk about what he has read, checking to see how much he remembers. This will help him to get thought from printed words and to comprehend their meaning. To help him recall facts, ask questions such as, "What happened first? Next? How do you think this story will end?"

6. Teach the child the vocabulary words he needs to know, five at a time, always keeping five pages beyond the page he is then reading.

7.   Remember to continue teaching your child to sound and write three-letter, short vowel words. (There are lists of short vowel words in Part Three of this book.)

8.   Lessons should not be longer than one half hour or, at most, forty-five minutes.

Begin each day's lesson with a review of the last five or ten vocabulary words he has been asked to learn. If he knows these words, select five more for him to learn. Have him read and reread two or, at most, three pages of his preprimer. Remember to have him read the short vowel chart. End the lesson with a game or an activity that will build up his phonetic word skills, such as telling him to make words using his lower-case letters or showing him pictures of objects that are spelled with three letters, such as dog, cat, wig, rug, and bed, and asking him to write their names.

Do not ask a child to sit still throughout a lesson. Now and then give him a chance to relax by asking him to get something for you or have him stand up while he says a word list. Never scold. Build up the child's ego by praising him, but do not say he has done well if he has done poorly. Instead say, "We'll keep working at this until you get better." Children learn best if they are enjoying what they are doing.

Occasionally a child is unable to master the reading vocabulary fast enough to learn the words for the pages he will soon be asked to read. If this happens, go to the library, select a very easy-to-read book, and have him read from it instead of his preprimer. If he comes to a word he has not learned, say it immediately for him. When he has mastered the vocabulary words for the next five pages in the basic preprimer, have him resume reading from it.

A child may read a page and remember nothing he has read. This is because he is so involved in the process of looking at words and recalling their names that he does not connect them to their meaning. Follow this four-step process of oral reading instruction:

1. Child reads.
2. Parent or tutor reads.
3. Child rereads.

4. The two of you talk about it. This procedure helps the child develop good comprehension.

When the child is halfway through the third preprimer, take the primer's word list to the printer. Have the words photocopied and enlarged to the size of the words in the primer's stories. Mount them on cards and on the back of each one write the page on which the word first occurs.

Use more of each day's lesson on vocabulary drill so the child can finish learning the preprimer's words and then learn the new words on the first twelve pages of the primer.

Writing: Manuscript

The handwriting taught in the first and second grades is a form of printing called manuscript. It is important that the child develop legible handwriting. He should be taught to shape letters properly, to make them the same size and at somewhat the same slant, and to space them evenly.

Do not encourage the child to write small. If he writes small, his writing will become cramped and hard to read. The lines on first-grade writing tablets are seven-eighths of an inch wide, and those on second-grade tablets three-fourths of an inch wide, usually with faint lines midway between each line to help the child gauge the height of lower-case letters, such as **a**, **e**, **h**, and **p**.

Encourage the child to hold his pencil correctly between his thumb and forefinger. The forefinger should be curved, not pressed hard against the pencil. If the child is right-handed, the eraser of his pencil should point to his right shoulder, and the top of his writing sheet should be slanted to the left. If he is left-handed, the eraser should point to his left shoulder, and his writing sheet should be slanted to the right.

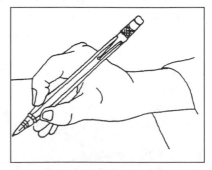

If the young child's fine motor skills have been slow in developing, he may find writing very difficult indeed. A small chalkboard is an excellent place to practice because it is easy to make lines on a chalkboard to guide the child when he is forming letters. To do this you need only a yardstick, white chalk, and crayons. With the yardstick, draw five horizontal chalk lines, each spaced four inches apart across the chalkboard. Then, with a white crayon, draw a line on top of each chalk line. Erase the chalk lines.

Next draw a chalk line just two inches below each white crayon line. Along each of the chalk lines draw a line with a blue crayon. Erase the chalk lines. You will now have a perfect place for the child to practice. He should write on the white crayon lines and use the midway blue crayon lines for spacing. Letters such as **b, l,** and **h** should be as tall as the space between the white lines; letters such as **a, e,** and **w** should touch the blue line. The lower sections of the **g, p,** and **y** should touch the blue line below. Teach the child to make letters the proper height.

Be sure to show the child how to shape each letter. He must be taught the direction of each curve the pencil line should take. Before he begins to write a letter, guide his hand as he "writes" the letter in space, then observe closely the motions he makes when he first writes it. Writing letters several times slowly and correctly makes them easier to learn. It is difficult to unlearn improper motions. Manuscript workbooks can be purchased at school supply stores. You will find a manuscript alphabet in Part Three of this book.

The Primer

Praise your child for having finished the preprimers. Tell him he is making real progress, that it is wonderful he is now ready to read a hardcover book.

Begin each lesson with a review of the last ten words learned. Have the child shuffle them, saying them three times, then putting them into a group labeled "(child's name) knows these." Continue teaching the vocabulary words used on the next five pages beyond the page the child is then reading. If there are words he has not yet mastered, make them a part of the next five-word group he is to learn.

You will probably find that it will take him at least three days to learn a five-word group. If it takes longer, do not be upset. Praise him for trying. Instead of reading new pages in the primer, have him choose and reread pages from stories he has already read, thus giving him time to learn the needed vocabulary words.

As soon as the child's first reading of a page becomes fairly smooth, ask him to tell you about what he has just read. If he can do this, change the reading order to:

1. Child reads.
2. He talks about the story.
3. Parent or tutor reads.
4. Child rereads.

Continue using the paper strip to help the child keep his place on the page and train his eyes to move from left to right. Do not drop your reading and the child's second reading of a page too soon. Dyslexics and children with reading disabilities usually need this practice all the way through the primer and the first-grade books.

In each day's lesson, include drills on sounding, spelling, and writing three-letter, short vowel words. Ask the child to say the short and long vowels on the picture strip frequently. (a—apple—a, e—egg—e, i—Indian—i, o—octopus—o, u—umbrella—u)

If a child has learned all the vocabulary words on twelve pages beyond the page he is reading, give him a five-word group of words from the Most Used Words list to learn. When he has mastered the A group, proceed to the B group, but remember to play a game with the A group occasionally, perhaps every other week until the child is sure of the words on it. Continue to teach the Most Used Words at a rate the child is able to master them. Do not expect him to learn these words quickly. If he knows half of them by the time he has completed reading the first-grade books, he has done well.

Begin each lesson with a review of the vowel sounds, then teach consonant sounds and sight words. Pace your teaching to the child's learning speed. If he is having difficulty learning vocabulary words, read only one new primer page a day and reread two pages. Reading two pages a day is just right for many children, but now and then a child may enjoy reading three pages. Remember to follow this order:

1. Child reads a page.
2. He talks about the story.
3. Tutor reads it.
4. The child rereads the page.

I do not advise teaching more than three primer pages a day. If the child wants to read more than this, take him to the public library and help him select "fun books" to read.

When the child has only twenty or thirty pages in the primer left to read, have the first-grade reader's word list photocopied and enlarged to the size of the words in its stories. Mount the words on cards and on each card's back write the number of the page on which the word first occurs. While the child is reading the last pages in his primer, teach him the vocabulary words he will need when he begins to read the first-grade reader.

The First-Grade Reader

Praise the child for finishing the primer, and hand him the first-grade reader. Give him time to leaf through it and talk about its pictures. Tell him he already knows many of the words in it.

Ask him to read the first two pages, sliding the paper strip down the page as he reads. Follow the same routine you were using when he read the primer:

1. The child reads a page.
2. He talks about what he has just read. (You might ask him what he thinks will happen next.)
3. If he is not reading fluently, you read the page.
4. The child rereads it.

Your method of teaching actually changes little. Each day have him say the five vocabulary words he has been asked to learn. Remove those he knows and replace them with vocabulary words he needs to learn, keeping the total to be learned at five words.

You will probably find he already knows some of the vocabulary words in the book's list. Put these in a stack labeled "(his name) knows these." The child will enjoy watching the stack grow.

Teach him the consonant digraphs, the consonant blends, and how to recognize and sound long vowel words. When introducing longer words, call attention to the fact that they are made up of syllables.

Include spelling in his daily lessons, three or four words from the Most Used Word lists, teaching them in the order in which they are listed. Beginning with the first one on a list, have him write each word as you pronounce it. If he misspells a word, circle it on your list. As soon as you have circled three or four words, stop and ask the child to learn how to spell them that week.

At the week's end, test him on the words you assigned by having him spell them orally and writing them, then pronounce words from the list until you have circled another three or four for next week's lesson. Once a week, retest him on those you have circled until he writes them automatically. Do not assign new words to be learned if he fails to remember those he has studied. Reassign the ones missed so he can master them, then resume checking his spelling of new words on the list. Dictate very short sentences made from words he has learned.

It is my hope that parents will have begun teaching the child to spell these common words while he was reading the primer. Proceed slowly, pronouncing the words in the order given on the lists. At first assign only three words a week, going on to perhaps five when he has finished the primer and is reading the first grade reader.

Encourage the child to write short stories three or four sentences long. Read his story with enthusiasm, expressing your delight. No doubt words will be misspelled and capitals will be absent. Sentences may end without periods. If you call attention to all these errors at once, he will be loath to ever write a story again. Have him read it to you. Then you may point out two or at most three related errors. If the sentences did not begin with capitals, call attention to that and to the fact that there should be periods at the sentences' ends. On later stories call attention to the spelling of one or two easy-to-sound words.

In the early grades, building a love for creative writing is more important than punctuation and spelling. By carefully teaching these skills in the child's early lessons, you will not destroy his love of creative writing.

Introduce all new concepts slowly, only one or two at a time. Never rush ahead. Make sure the child understands and is able to use each phonics fact you have been teaching before introducing a new one. Throughout your teaching of the first-grade reader you will probably need to call attention to previously learned phonics facts daily.

Be sure to have the child read and reread two pages orally every day. If a child reads less than this, he makes little progress.

Remember to select the second-grade readers and prepare the first

second-grade reader's vocabulary cards a few weeks before the child finishes the first-grade reader.

Consonant Digraphs

A digraph is made up of two letters that have been given a single
sound. The **ch** in church, **sh** in shoe, **wh** in wheel, **th** in think, and the **th**
in then are consonant digraphs. The **ch** in school and the **ph** in phone are
also digraphs; call attention to these when you introduce words that contain them.

Print these digraphs on small squares of heavy paper, and cut out
small pictures of objects that have these initial sounds. (In Part Three of
this book there are pictures of objects whose names begin with digraphs.)

Begin with the two digraphs **sh** and **ch**. Place the pictures of six
objects beginning with **ch** (such as chin, chair, child, church, chick, and
chimney) and six objects beginning with **sh** (such as ship, shark, shovel,
shoe, shirt, and sheep) on the table in front of the child.

Tell him that **ch** sounds like an old train starting up, "Ch, ch—ch, ch,
ch." Pretend you are both imitating trains, "Ch, ch—-ch, ch, ch." When
the child is sure of the sound of the digraph **ch**, point to pictures of the
objects that begin with it and have him practice, saying them while emphasizing the digraph: "Ch, chin; ch, chair; ch, child; ch, church; ch, chick;
ch, chimney."

Introduce the sound of **sh** by placing your index finger on your lips
and saying, "Sh, sh, be quiet." Have the child repeat the sound, then say
the names of these pictures emphasizing the digraph **sh**: "Sh, ship; sh,
shark; sh, shovel; sh, shoe; sh, shirt; sh, sheep."

Mix up the pictures of the objects. Ask the child to pick up each picture and spell its initial digraph as he places it beneath the square labeled
"ch" or "sh."

When you introduce the digraph **wh**, tell the child this one actually
sounds like **hw**. Sound the **h** and **w**, one after the other rapidly. Emphasize
this sound as you and the child say the names of pictures beginning with
the digraph **wh**: "wh, wheel; wh, whale; wh, whip; wh, wheelchair; wh,
whistle." Laugh with the child about this digraph being spelled backward.

Mix these pictures with those beginning with **ch** and **sh**, and cut out
other small pictures of objects with these initial digraphs. Make a game

of having them placed in columns beneath their labels. Ask, "Which digraph now has the most pictures? That one is the winner."

Last of all, introduce the two sounds of the digraph **th**. Use pictures and numbers for the **th** sound: th, thumb; th, throat; th, thermometer; th, thimble; th, 3, th, 13, and th, 30.

Mix these pictures in with those used for the other digraphs and have the child make a game of sorting them under their labels "**ch**," "**sh**," "**wh**," and "**th**."

After the child has mastered these sounds, call attention to the slightly different sound of the **th** in these vocabulary words: them, this, that, these, then, and those. Tell him that if one of the **th** sounds doesn't "unlock" a word, he should try the other.

Some children learn the sounds of the consonant digraphs quickly, others need special help. Be patient, the child will eventually master them.

Consonant Blends

Two or three consonants are often blended together. When they are said together almost like one sound, they are called consonant blends. These words begin with consonant blends: **bl**, black; **cl**, clap; **fl**, flag; **pl**, play; **sl**, slip; **spl**, splash; **sc**, scare; **sk**, skin; **sm**, small; **st**, step; **str**, street; **sw**, swim; **tw**, twin; **br**, bread; **dr**, drum; **gr**, grass; **cr**, cry; **fr**, frog; **tr**, tree; **spr**, spray.

Many words end with consonant blends. Some children find ending blends harder to learn: **nd**, hand; **nk**, bank, **ng**, sang; **lb**, bulb; **lp**, help; **lk**, milk; **mp**, camp; **ft**, gift; **lt**, felt; **nt**, went; **pt**, kept; **ct**, fact; **st**, best; **sk**, desk.

Print these words on flash cards and have the child learn to say them a few at a time. Begin with the initial blends. When introducing vocabulary words, call attention to blends in them. (There are lists of blends in Part Three of this book.)

Long Vowel Words

As soon as your child has learned to sound the three-letter, short vowel words easily, introduce him to the long vowel words. Have him memorize this rule: "When two vowels go walking, the first vowel does the talking. It says its alphabet name. The second vowel says nothing."

Explain the meaning of this rule. Tell the child the word coat has two vowels. The first vowel, o, says its long name, o. The a is silent. The two vowels do not have to be next to each other. The word like has two vowels. The first vowel, i, says its name. The e says nothing; it is silent.

Put these words on flash cards:

Long a   bait, late, care, pain, cave, mail, chair, name, wait, wake
Long e   bead, tree, these, year, sheep, Pete, bean, sweet, tea, beak
Long i   like, fine, smile, drive, hide, five, shine, kite, slide, wife
Long o   rope, boat, hole, vote, stone, goes, woke, snore, coat, froze
Long u   cute, mule, pure, use, cube. The vowel u also has the sound you hear in rule, tune, and flute.

Some very short words have only one vowel, and it is at the word's end. The vowel in these words is long. If the word ends in y, the y has the sound of long i. Examples: my, be, she, hi, by, me, why, go.

When the child seems to have mastered this concept, have him read this list of words for review: fat, fate, kit, kite, set, seat, rip, ripe, slid, slide, rod, rode, hop, hope, lad, laid, bet, beat, at, ate, red, read, cot, cote, rack, rake, sell, seal, jut, jute. (There are lists of long and short vowel words in Part Three of this book. Use them to make flash cards.)

If the child is slow in noting whether vowels are long or short, mix the short and long vowel flash cards together. Hand him the pack. Ask him to say each word's vowel sound. As he lays the word card down, you say the word. Continue this process, making a game of it. If he misses a vowel sound, his invisible friend, Jack, gets the card. See who wins.

The Letters W and Y

W and y are consonants when they are at the beginning of words or syllables. They are often used as vowels at the end of words.

W is a vowel in these words that end with the long o sound: snow, blow, show, and crow.

Y has the long sound of i when it ends very short words, such as by, cry, my, and why.

Y has the long sound of **e** when it ends words that have more than one syllable. Examples: happy (hap py), funny (fun ny), sleepy (sleep y), city (cit y), pony (po ny), kitty (kit ty), candy (can dy).

Introducing Syllables

Long words are easier to read and spell if they are divided into their smaller parts. These parts are called syllables. There is always at least one vowel in every syllable.

You may ask, "When should I teach the child to notice syllables?" Begin when he is reading the primer and the first-grade reading book. Tap the table with your pencil or clap your hands to the rhythm of the syllables in familiar words. Have the child clap his name. Make a game of it.

The child may find placing his hand flat under his chin helpful in detecting the number of syllables in a word. Do this exercise with the child as you slowly say, "Place your hand out in front of you, palm down, thumb under, and fingers straight. Now put your hand under your chin. Say 'story.' How many syllables do you feel?"

"Two."

"Try this word, 'tomorrow'."

"Three."

Continue with other words: strawberry, children, number, remember, under, and so forth.

In primers and first-grade readers there are many two-syllable words, such as cowboy, airplane, forgot, besides, uphill, today, into, birthday, and something. There are words that end with the suffixes **ing**, **es**, **est**, **er**, **en**, **ful**, and **ly**. For example: going, boxes, tallest, smaller, taken, thankful, quickly.

When you introduce the reading lesson's vocabulary, call attention to the words that have two or more syllables. Print the words with spaces between the syllables thus: air plane, birth day, box es, thank ful. When introducing a two-syllable word on a flash card, cover the last syllable with your finger as you say the first syllable. Then cover the first syllable as you say the last one.

Teaching the child to see syllables will help him recognize words quickly, as well as aid him in learning to spell them.

Between Reading Books

When a child with a reading disability has finished the first-grade reader, he is often still reading word-for-word because of slow word recall. Even though he has worked very hard memorizing the basic vocabulary in his reader, going immediately to the next reader may make word recall even more difficult and frustrating. Do not let him become discouraged. Tell him it will be easier for him to remember the words if he reads another book before going on to the second-grade reader.

Go to the public library and ask the librarian to help you select an easy-to-read book at primer or middle-first-grade level, a book thirty or forty pages long. Select one on a subject your child is interested in— sports, dinosaurs, mysteries, or any other subject.

Many easy-to-read books end with word lists. Take the book to a quick-print shop. Show the printer the size of the words in the book's stories and have the list photocopied, enlarging them to that size. Cut the word list apart. Discard words you are sure the child already knows and affix the remaining words to cards with Scotch tape. Write the page number on which the word first occurs on the back of each card, then stack the vocabulary cards in that order.

Continue daily reading lessons as before. Teach five new vocabulary words and reteach the words the child is slow in recalling. Have him read each page aloud, helping him with the sentences that he finds difficult, and ask him to reread the page. When he has finished reading a page, talk about what has happened in the story. Reading two or three pages daily in this way will speed up his word recall and develop his comprehension.

You need not have the child read the entire book. As soon as his word recall has improved and he is reading somewhat smoothly, go on to the second-grade level.

Vacation Times

If you are taking a vacation, or if you feel the child needs a rest from his daily lessons, do not let him discontinue reading. Children with reading disabilities should read something every day. Even when a week goes by without reading, the dyslexic's ability to read slips backward.

Take your child to the library. Ask the librarian to help you locate "fun" books for him in the easy-to-read section. Be sure he can read the books you select. When reading aloud, he should not miss more than three words out of one hundred. If he does, the book is too difficult. Help him find an easier book. (When counting words missed do not include proper nouns.)

During the vacation, have him read two or three pages aloud to you each day from his library book. When he hesitates, count one, two, three slowly to yourself, then quickly supply the word. Do not have him sound the words; he is reading for pleasure. Talk and laugh about the story he is reading. By having the child read every day you will keep him from slipping backward.

I do not advise taking long and too frequent vacations from daily reading lessons. If a vacation is longer than two weeks, the child may forget too many of his vocabulary words.

The Second-Grade Readers

There are two second-grade readers—one for the first half of the second grade and another for the last half. I hope that you have been able to secure books of the same series you used in the first grade. If not, select only readers that have word lists and easy, familiar words, not readers with uncommon words and difficult names.

Remember to prepare each book's vocabulary cards a few weeks before the child finishes his current reader. Vocabulary word cards for readers in grades one and two are very necessary. They are usually also necessary for grade three.

Take the book's word list to the printer. Have the words photocopied and enlarged to the same size as those on the first-grade reader's vocabulary cards. Mount them on cards and on each card's back write the number of the page on which the word will first occur. Arrange the cards in order according to page number. Teach the child the words that will occur on the first six pages of the first second-grade reader.

If the second-grade books are of a different series, when the child encounters an unfamiliar word in his reading jot it down, print it on a card, and add it to his reading vocabulary.

The method of teaching the second-grade readers is a continuation of that used for the first-grade reader. There are only very gradual changes to be made as the child develops his reading skills. Always pay close attention to sight-word vocabulary development, phonetic skills, oral reading, and comprehension. Have the child continue to slide the paper strip under each line as he reads; this will strengthen his left-to-right eye movements.

Plan Each Week's Lessons

Set aside time at the beginning of each week to plan that week's lessons.

1. Select the vocabulary words the child needs to learn. Before he is asked to read from the basic reader, he must know the words on that page. If he does not know 98 percent of them, he will become very frustrated and may lose faith in himself; therefore you must find out which vocabulary words he still does not know. Ask him to say the group of sight words he has been studying. File those he knows with those labeled "(child's name) knows these." Put aside the words he has not mastered and include these with the words he is to learn that week.

Take out the reader's vocabulary word cards. Lay them down, word-side up one at a time, having the child say the word if he knows it. Stack the cards in order in two stacks, those he knows and those he does not know. When there are ten or fifteen cards in the stack he does not know, form them into groups of five. Put a rubber band around each group. These are the sight words he is to learn that week. Teach them in the order they first appear in the reader.

Now you can plan the lessons without him being present. Check the number on the last card to see if these will supply the vocabulary sight words that will occur on the next fifteen pages of his book. If they do not, plan to have the child reread his favorite stories that week and only two new pages in his book. This will give him time to master needed vocabulary words.

If the number on the last card is more than twenty-five pages beyond the page he is reading, assign only ten words or assign sight words from the Most Used Word lists instead of the reader's vocabulary words.

2. On a strip of stiff paper (2″ wide and 10″ long), write the numbers of the pages he is to read aloud each day.

Example:	Mon.	Thur.
	p. 25, 26	Reread p. 15, 16
	Tues.	Fri.
	p. 27, 28	p. 17, 18
	Wed.	Sat.
	p. 29, 30	p. 19, 20

Make sure the child reads and rereads at least two pages each day, otherwise he will make little progress. If the child is mastering the sight words easily, assign three pages twice a week and two pages on the other four days. Use the paper strip, one side for a bookmark and the other side for sliding down the page when reading. Always save time to check comprehension, pausing at the end of each page to let the child retell in detail what happened on that page.

3. Plan to teach one phonetic fact each week. In Part Three of this book there are word charts to be used in teaching the phonetic skills. These are arranged in the order in which they should be taught. Review the phonetic principles the child is not remembering to use or seems to have forgotten. In first grade the child should have learned how to sound short and long vowel words, consonant blends, and consonant digraphs. Frequently these phonetic principles need to be reviewed in the second grade. It is very important that he master them. Save part of each day's lesson for teaching and reviewing phonetic skills.

Purchase a small spiral notebook—shorthand wide-line notebooks are excellent—and number the pages. In the back of the notebook write the phonetic facts you plan to teach the coming week and the week's spelling lesson—five to eight sight words from the Most Used Words list.

In the front of the notebook print the phonetic principles he has been taught, one to a page. Each time you teach a new phonetic principle, print it on a page in the notebook. Include a few examples beside each definition and have the child add a few more. When a child seems to have forgotten a rule, have him look it up in this notebook and give examples of its meaning. When you teach a new syllabication principle, print it on a page together with examples that show its meaning.

In second grade the child should learn diphthongs, the r-controlled vowels, and the hard and soft sounds of **c** and **g**. He should learn more about dividing words into syllables and be taught how to recognize and spell the following suffixes and word endings: **ed**, **er**, **est**, **ing**, **ly**, **ful**, **less**, **ness**, **ment**, **tion**, and **_le** (as in peo ple and ta ble).

On the following pages, how to teach these phonetic and syllabication principles is explained in detail. (The page number for each skill is listed in Part Two's table of contents.)

Daily Lessons

1. Most serious dyslexics in this grade are still reading slowly, hesitating now and then to recall words they are sure they know. Reading orally at least two pages a day will speed up the child's word recall. Have him read each page aloud to get its content. Ask him to tell you in detail what he has just read, then have him reread the page to develop fluency.

When his reading has become fairly smooth, you may occasionally tell him to read a paragraph or a short, easy page silently, then talk about it and reread it aloud.

At first the child will probably move his lips when he reads silently; this usually happens—don't call his attention to it. If the sentences are long, he may not be able to tell you what he just read. Do not let him become frustrated. Have him read the page orally and then talk about it with him. Develop this skill very gradually by having him silently read portions of stories he finds interesting. Remember, he has been reading orally using two senses, sight and sound. When he reads silently, he uses only one sense, seeing, to comprehend the meaning of printed words.

The teaching of reading is a developmental process. Often the child's reading improves so slowly you feel no progress is being made. Hang in there, and be patient. The day will come when, to your surprise and your child's great pleasure, he realizes he knows how to unlock new words and is able to read with a degree of fluency.

2. Ask the child to write a story each week. Help him decide what to write about, then tell him to write the story himself, not during the regular lesson time. If he asks you how to spell an uncommon word, spell it for him. If it is a word he can find easily in the dictionary, help him look it up.

Some children love to write stories; others find writing them very difficult. If a child dislikes writing, teach him to write very short stories three or four sentences long. Meanwhile improve his sentence-writing ability by dictating two or three sentences as a part of his spelling lesson using words he has previously learned to spell.

Always praise the child's stories. Be content with correcting only a few errors. Do not discourage him. Call attention to capitals, punctuation, and the spelling of common words, correcting only two or three items at a time. Improvement is usually very gradual.

3. As a part of one day's lesson, teach the child the friendly letter writing form. Tell him there is a special pattern used when writing to a friend. If possible, show him a letter you have received, calling attention to the date on the right at its top, the salutation, body, ending, and signature.

Let the child decide to whom he wishes to write. It may be a playmate who has moved away or a thank you letter to a grandparent.

On unlined paper draw the framework for a short friendly letter, making your lines far enough apart to accommodate the child's handwriting. Have him fill in the form, writing in the date, "Dear _____," a two or three sentence message, followed by "Your friend" or "With love" at the end. Have him sign it. Show him how to address the envelope and where to place the stamp. Be sure to mail it.

FRIENDLY LETTER FORM

(Date)_____

Dear _____,

_____

_____

_____

_____

Your friend,

(Name)_____

4. Get into the habit of taking the child to the library frequently. Help him select books on subjects that interest him. Make sure they are easy— easier than his reading book. There should be no more than two unfamiliar words in every one hundred, not counting names.

Encourage the child to read on his own. When he asks you a word, say it for him immediately. Do not make him think reading is work by having him "sound out" every word he does not know. Listen when he talks about what he has read, and praise him lavishly when he finishes a book.

5. When the child is about to complete the second second-grade reader (fifty pages from its end), select readers for the third grade. If possible, use books from the same series. Have the word lists photocopied and enlarged to the size of the print in the reader and prepare the third-grade readers' vocabulary cards. While the child is finishing the second-grade reader, teach him the vocabulary words that will occur on the first ten pages of the first third-grade reader.

Dyslexics and children with serious reading problems should read and reread at least two pages daily the year round. They should be encouraged to read "fun books" during vacations. If they fail to read for a week or two their word recall weakens, and they begin to lose their reading skills.

Spelling

Many dyslexics find spelling very difficult. They study the week's spelling words nightly, get an A or B on that week's test, and forget how to spell the same words in one or two weeks. Frequently they are unable to write sentences because they cannot spell common words correctly.

It is important to teach the child to spell the lists of the Most Used Words. (These lists are in Part Three of this book.) Pace your teaching to the child's ability to learn to spell. Make sure he is able to spell every word on each list. If he can spell all of the Most Used Words by the time he finishes the second-grade readers, he has done well. If he continues misspelling certain words, have him write them in his notebook so he can look them up quickly when he is writing.

Some people feel that writing a word ten or twenty times is the right way to learn to spell it. I do not find this to be true. Rather, it very well may be the way to ruin the child's handwriting as well as make him feel that learning to spell is impossible.

At the beginning of the week, pronounce his entire spelling list to ascertain which words he finds difficult, then drill on these words nightly.

Try taping a list of the difficult words on the bathroom mirror or refrigerator door so he can review them himself.

Have the child spell the words aloud, then write them, calling attention to the phonics rules that apply to their vowel sounds. Note the words that contain schwas. Often it helps to make up a chant to emphasize the schwa's spelling in such words. Example: Chant the word separate, changing the schwa in its middle syllable to a long a. Say: "sep a rate, sep a rate, sep a rate," emphasizing the a.

Pronounce the entire list of words the night before the end-of-the-week test. Have him write them and restudy the missed words. Never tell him he is stupid because he has difficulty learning to spell simple words. Praise him when he looks in the dictionary to see how a word is spelled.

Many English words can be spelled by sounding them and writing the letter or letters that stand for each sound. Help the child discover that the same phonics rules he used in learning to read words will help him spell them. Write important phonics rules in his notebook and have him review them often.

Learning to Use the Dictionary

Book stores have many types of dictionaries for sale. Children's one-book dictionaries, based on the reading they are to do in elementary grades, are best. These dictionaries are for children in grades one through five, and every child who has a reading disability needs this type of dictionary.

Introduce the child to his dictionary. Have him open it and look for a very common word, such as cat, zoo, or milk.

Help him to realize that knowing how to alphabetize helps him locate words in many books. Get the telephone book and help him look up his telephone number. Look up a subject interesting to him in an encyclopedia.

Each of the words listed below begin with different letters. Use this list for teaching alphabetizing: child, ghost, left, hour, plan, mouth, own, wave, ruler, tool. Ask the child to write the numbers one to ten in a column. Have him say the alphabet, stopping after each letter to see if there is a word beginning with that letter. If one occurs, he is to write its initial letter as follows:

1.	c	6.	o
2.	g	7.	p
3.	h	8.	r
4.	l	9.	t
5.	m	10.	w

When all the initial letters have been written, have him finish writing the words.

When the child has learned to alphabetize different initial letter words easily, introduce groups of two words beginning with the same initial. Ask him to alphabetize this list of words: circle, fin, horse, goat, raft, music, heart, child, record, globe, flower, money. The child should now be able to write the initial letters without help. His beginning chart should look like this:

1.	c	7.	h
2.	c	8.	h
3.	f	9.	m
4.	f	10.	m
5.	g	11.	r
6.	g	12.	r

Next ask him to write the second letter of each group, making sure the second letters are in alphabetical order.

1.	ch	7.	he
2.	ci	8.	ho
3.	fi	9.	mo
4.	fl	10.	mu
5.	gl	11.	ra
6.	go	12.	re

Tell him to finish spelling the words.

Make up other lists of similar groups. When the child has learned to alphabetize these easily, ask him to alphabetize this list of words using the same method, looking at the third or fourth letter of each word: due, bank, dye, jet, cold, jerk, bark, dust, comb, bath, nerve, pulp, truck, nest, snag, puff, wind, punch, true, window, snake.

If the child can alphabetize this list without help, he is ready to look up words in the dictionary. Tell him that knowing the alphabet really well will make it possible for him to look up words quickly. Have him practice opening the dictionary to the part where he'll probably find that letter of the alphabet. Letters a through f are in the front part of the dictionary, letters g through p in the middle, and q through z are toward the back. Teach him to use the guide words at the top of each page.

Help the child form the habit of looking up words and facts. Invent dictionary games. Whenever the child expresses interest in a topic, take time to help him look it up in an encyclopedia and talk about it. The child with a reading disability not only needs to use a dictionary to enlarge his vocabulary, but very often he needs to refer to it for help in spelling.

Diphthongs

A diphthong is a gliding speech sound. The gliding vowel sounds we hear in boy, cow, few, hawk, and good are diphthongs, and these are used in many words. The child must learn to quickly recognize and say them, just as he has learned to say short and long vowels. Teach this list of diphthongs one group at a time. Put these words on flash cards and review them making sure the child knows them well:

oi, oy	oil, coin, boil, join, soil, toy, joy, boy
ou, ow	out, loud, found, cloud, town, flower, plow, owl
au, aw	haul, Paul, auto, paw, straw, saw, lawn
oo (as in book)	foot, good, hook, wool
oo (as in moon)	soon, cool, zoo, tooth, booth
ew	few, chew, flew, knew

There are lists of diphthongs in Part Three of this book.

r-Controlled Vowels

Er, ir, and **ur** have the sound you hear in herd, girl, and burn. Teach these words calling attention to the fact that we cannot tell how the word is spelled by its r-controlled sound. Knowing the sounds of the letters helps us spell many words correctly, but there are some words that we must learn to spell. Examples: her, bird, hurt, fern, shirt, fur, jerk, dirt, curb, clerk, firm, curl.

The **ar** in many words has the sound you hear in the word are. The **or** has the same sound you hear in the word ore. Teach these lists of words:

> **ar** arm, car, bar, yard, bark, start, jar
> **or** for, torn, born, fork, sports, corn, porch

There are lists of words with r-controlled vowels in Part Three of this book.

The Soft and Hard Sounds of C and G

The letter **c** has the soft sound of **s** if it is followed by an **e**, **i**, or **y**. Examples: city, race, cell, cent, pencil, rice, cinder, cyclone.

If the letter **c** is followed by any other letter except **ch**, as in church, it has the hard sound of **k**. Examples: cake, clap, cop, cook, crash, cut.

Call attention to the soft and hard sounds in these words: bicycle, circus, circle.

The letter **g** usually has the soft sound of **j** when followed by an **e**, **i**, or **y**. Examples: giant, age, huge, page, gym, cage, ginger, gem, stingy.

The letter **g** has the hard sound when followed by other letters, and also when it is at the end of a word. Examples: glad, game, good, goat, grass, gun, flag, bag.

The sound of the **g** in these common words does not follow the soft **g** rule: get, give, gift, girl. If the child notices this, tell him these are exceptions to the soft **g** rule.

There are lists of words that have the soft and hard sounds of **c** and **g** in Part Three of this book.

Phonics Review

There are many other rules used in sounding words; however, most children find too many rules confusing and tiresome. I have given you phonics rules that I feel are essential. Dyslexics need them because it is often difficult for them to immediately recall words, even those they know well. Knowing the sounds of letters, digraphs, and diphthongs[1] enables them to recall words quickly.

If you do not constantly emphasize these important phonics rules, your child will never learn to use them. Teach these rules, one at a time, reviewing them often. Do not rush. Introducing a new rule before the child really understands those you've been teaching will confuse him. If he has learned to use all of these rules by the time he is reading at the third-grade level, he has done very well indeed.

Never forget to teach the child the needed reading vocabulary before beginning the oral reading lesson—sight words are very important to dyslexics. Also try to take a little time at the end of each day's lesson to review and teach phonics rules.

Cursive Writing

Children are introduced to cursive writing in the last part of second grade. Writing books that show how the shape of each manuscript letter is changed to cursive can be purchased at school supply stores. These books help the child to understand how the letters are shaped and make it easier for him to learn to read this type of handwriting.

A chalkboard that has been lined for writing is an excellent place for the child to practice cursive. Guide his hand as he "writes" a letter in space several times before actually having him write it. After he has written several letters, call attention to their shape, slant, size, and proper spacing.

Before the child begins to write in his writing book, have him trace lightly over the letters several times, then have him practice writing the letters on the wide-line paper used in the second-grade. (The lines on this paper are three-fourths of an inch wide.) When he is ale to write the letters correctly, he can copy them into his writing book.

Paper with lines one-half inch wide is best for third graders. Some school supply stores sell tablets with lines of this width divided midway

---

1. See contents, Part Two, for the page numbers on which consonant digraphs and diphthongs are explained.

with dotted lines. These are a real help to the child learning to write cursive.

After a month or two in the third grade, the child may be asked to do all his written assignments in cursive writing. Encourage him to write carefully. Tell him that if he forms each letter correctly, his good writing will become automatic, he will gain speed, and his writing will be easy to read. (You will find a cursive alphabet in Part Three of this book.)

The Third-Grade Readers

My friend, who had been teaching eighth grade for several years, decided to teach the third grade instead. She felt certain that in the third grade she could help children perfect their reading, language, spelling, and study skills. They would then have the skills necessary for successfully completing junior high and high school. She was right—the children she taught in third grade did well in the upper grades.

In the second grade children are taught phonetic rules and words. Some children easily master these, but others use only a few of the phonetic skills they are taught and have only vague ideas of syllabication. Many move their lips when they are reading silently and whisper their words.

Oral reading should be continued in the third grade until the child is able to recall vocabulary words easily, then he should be encouraged to read silently. Constant attention should be paid to vocabulary buildup. The child should be encouraged to look up words in the dictionary and read for enjoyment. Reading only the basic reader is not enough; the child who reads many books of interest will develop a good vocabulary.

If possible, the time set aside for tutoring the child in the third grade should be increased to one hour each day. If the child tires easily, plan two half-hour periods. The lesson should include reading vocabulary, phonics, syllabication, and reading for comprehension.

Saying words is not reading. Getting the intended thought from written sentences and paragraphs is reading. The most important part of each day's lesson is the development of comprehension skills. Learning to read and follow directions, to understand questions and find their answers, to locate facts, to distinguish between details and main ideas, to make outlines, and to report on subjects of interest are comprehension skills the child should master in the third grade.

Following Directions

The child may get wrong answers because he does not realize the importance of reading and following directions. Purchase a third-grade phonics workbook from a school supply store or your school. Have the child read the directions and explain to you what he will do before he begins filling in the blanks on each page.

If he does not understand what he is supposed to do, have him reread the page; he should learn to read directions before starting to fill in blanks. If the concept being introduced is new to him, explain it before he begins to read the directions. Do not continue to explain the same thing page after page. Instead, ask him to tell you what he thinks the directions mean, and if necessary have him reread the page on which that concept was introduced.

If the phonics page is completed incorrectly, have him reread the directions to find out why his answers are wrong. He must always correct every mistake, otherwise there is little learning.

There are directions on children's games, model kits, and other toys. Teach him to read the directions before he begins to play with a new toy.

Understanding Questions

Some children give wrong answers to questions because they do not properly read questions beginning with these words: **where, when, who, what, why,** and **how.** They may just be mispronouncing these words, or they may not understand their meanings.

Teach the child that:
>where is a place;
>when is a time;
>who is usually a person;
>what is a thing;
>why is a reason (because);
>how is the way a thing is done.

Write these six words with their meanings on a card, then make up sentences to illustrate them. Break each sentence into parts asking the child which word that part would answer.

Examples:

1. At lunch time the three boys ate the whole cake.
   When?   at lunch time
   Who?   the three boys
   What?   the whole cake
2. My little brother stayed in bed this morning because he
   was sick.
   Who?   my little brother
   Where?   in bed
   When?   this morning
   Why?   because he was sick
3. Because they were late, the two boys tiptoed quietly into
   their classroom.
   Why?   because they were late
   Who?   the two boys
   How?   quietly
   Where?   the classroom

Often a child cannot answer a question because it contains a word that is not in his vocabulary. Ask him to look up the word in the dictionary and read the meaning. If the dictionary gives several, help him select the right one. If he does not understand the dictionary's explanation, explain it to him. Help him reword the question using words he understands; then he can look for its answer.

Getting the Facts—Finding the Answers

Asking the child to tell you in detail what happened on the page he just read helps him get facts. Teaching him to locate clue words and antecedents will help him find the answers to questions.

1. *Clue Words*—Teach the child how to look for clue words to use when looking for the answers to a question. Ask him, "Which word or words in this question are clue words?" Then tell him to scan the page quickly for the clue word or words that have similar meaning. Tell him it is unnecessary to read word-for-word until he locates the clue words.

Instead, he should glance quickly over the page until he spies those words. To develop this ability, have the child scan, first for certain proper nouns and dates and then for particular words.

2. *Antecedents*—Teach the child how to find the antecedents of pronouns. An antecedent is the noun, pronoun, or the part of a sentence referred to by the pronoun. In the following paragraph the pronoun it appears two times. Each time it refers to a different fact.

> Brazil is the largest country in South America. It is almost as big as the United States of America. Most of the country lies in the tropics, where it is warm and wet.

The antecedent of the first it is "Brazil." The antecedent of the second it is "the tropics."

In the following paragraph there are three pronouns. The pronoun they appears twice, and the pronoun them, once.

> More than twenty animals are painted on the ceiling of the Altamira Cave in Spain. At first people did not believe they were prehistoric art. They said cave men were too stupid to paint them.

The antecedent of the first they is "more than twenty animals." The antecedent of the second they is "people." The antecedent of them is "more than twenty animals."

3. *Learning to Find Answers in Textbooks*—If the child finds social studies and science very difficult, have him bring these textbooks home two or three nights each week. Read the lessons with him. If the words are not in his reading vocabulary, read the paragraphs for him, stopping now and then for him to read the easy sentences. Stop after each section and ask him to retell, in his own words, the part that has just been read. If he doesn't understand its meaning explain it in simpler words.

Jot down the important vocabulary words and explain their meaning. Have the child use them in sentences, and review these words until he uses them easily. If there are questions at the end of a chapter, teach the child to find the clue words in the questions and then scan under the proper subtitle for the information needed. If he cannot find the clue word there, teach him to look for it in the index.

Main Ideas and Details

Being able to locate the main idea in a paragraph is an important comprehension skill. Develop this by asking the child to read a paragraph and tell you what it is mostly about. Tell him his answer should fit the whole paragraph, not just one part of it.

Some paragraphs have very clear main ideas. Select such a paragraph from a story the child is reading. Have him reread it and say what he thinks it is mostly about. Then ask him to count the number of details given that explain its main idea. Suppose he is reading this paragraph:

> Animals protect themselves in different ways. The rabbit, whose fur is the color of brown leaves, stays still. The turtle draws into its shell. The skunk squirts bad-smelling oil. The porcupine shoots quills.

The first sentence gives the main idea. The next four give details.

Some paragraphs contain one sentence that states the main idea. This sentence is called the topic sentence. Usually the topic sentence is the first or the last sentence in a paragraph. Ask the child to locate the topic sentence in this paragraph:

> In our country most holidays are celebrated on the same day in every state. This is not true of Arbor Day, the day set aside for planting trees. Florida celebrates Arbor Day in January, California in March, and Nebraska in April. Each state celebrates Arbor Day in the month that has the best climate for planting trees.

In this paragraph the topic sentence is the last sentence.

Many paragraphs, however, do not contain topic sentences. This paragraph does not have one:

> The common opossum lives in the United States. It is the size of a house cat, has a long snout, big ears, dark eyes, and rough grayish-white fur. Its long tail is almost hairless. It has fifty sharp teeth and sharp claws with widely separated toes.

Ask the child what he thinks this paragraph is mostly about. If he says, "the common opossum," agree that this is true, but tell him that in this paragraph the main idea is more definite. Is the paragraph mostly about the size of an opossum? Its long tail? Its sharp teeth and claws? The child will soon note that these are details. This paragraph tells what an opossum looks like. All but one of its sentences describe an opossum.

The social studies textbook is an excellent book to use for teaching the child to distinguish between main ideas and details. When you are helping the child with the day's assignment, watch for paragraphs that explain important concepts.

Suppose the child is studying about how our country began. The chapter he is reading is titled, "The Thirteen Original Colonies." He has been asked to find out why the colonies decided to break away from England and become a new nation. The chapter he is reading has three subtitles: "Unfair Laws," "The War Begins," and "Declaration of Independence."

Tell the child that each subtitle names a main idea that will explain why or how the thirteen colonies became a nation. Be sure he knows the meanings of these words: colonies, colonists, taxes, declaration, and independence. Read and talk about each part of the chapter; then have him retell in his own words the reason the colonies decided to become independent.

Locating main ideas and selecting supporting details are important study skills. When the child becomes adept at distinguishing between main ideas and details, he will find it easy to locate the correct answers to the questions in his social studies and science books.

Outlining

In the third-grade social studies and science classes children are required to give reports on special topics. Being able to prepare an outline to follow when giving an oral report is a necessary skill.

The child who knows how to locate main ideas and their supporting details will not find making outlines too difficult. He already knows a basic form is used when writing letters. Tell him a basic form is also used in outlining. Main ideas are numbered with Roman numerals, and beneath each main idea details are listed using capital letters instead of numbers. If there are facts to include about a detail, these are numbered 1, 2, 3, and so forth. If he does not know Roman numerals, have him memorize one through ten. (I, II, III, IV, V, VI, VII, VIII, IX, X.)

On a blank sheet of paper help him rule an outline form for three main ideas, each of which will have three details. Add spaces for two facts after detail C at the end. Emphasize the importance of properly indenting each part of the outline, and have him save his outline for future reference. It should look like this:

Subject: _____

I. _____

    A. _____

    B. _____

    C. _____

II. _____

    A. _____

    B. _____

    C. _____

III. _____

    A. _____

    B. _____

    C. _____

        1. _____

        2. _____

Ask the child to make a duplicate of this form for an outline on Japan. The subject is: Home Life, Education, and Recreation in Japan. Have the child write its subject on the top line. Each part is a main idea. Tell him to write "Home Life" after the Roman numeral I, "Education" after II, and "Recreation" after III, then complete the outline using the items listed below. There are three details for each main idea, and two facts that should be written after the last detail.

1. Schooling begins at age six.
2. Japanese read a great deal.
3. Japanese homes are clean and orderly.
4. Nearly everyone has a hobby.
5. Usually the wives decide what the families need.
6. Exams show when a child is ready to pass.
7. Japanese take part in many sports.
8. Children behave so that others will think well of their families.
9. They ski, bowl, and play golf.
10. Most young people finish high school.
11. Baseball is the favorite sport.

The finished outline should look like this:

Home Life, Education, and Recreation in Japan
  I. Home Life
    A.   Japanese homes are clean and orderly.
    B.   Usually the wives decide what the families need.
    C.   Children behave so that others will think well of their families.
 II. Education
    A.   Schooling begins at age six.
    B.   Exams show when a child is ready to pass.
    C.   Most young people finish high school.
III. Recreation
    A.   Japanese read a great deal.
    B.   Nearly everyone has a hobby.
    C.   Japanese take part in many sports.
        1.   They ski, bowl, and play golf.
        2.   Baseball is the favorite sport.

The next time the child is asked to give a report, help him locate information on it, then assist him in making an outline to follow when he is writing the report or giving it orally.

Writing Reports on Assigned Topics

To the child with a reading disability, writing a report may seem an impossible task. When his teacher asks him to write a science or social studies report, help him select a topic that interests him. Go with him to the children's section of the public library and show him how to locate the topic in an encyclopedia. Read the information together, talk about it, and help him make a simple outline, jotting down the necessary facts.

Tell him he must not copy the encyclopedia information word-for-word. Instead, he must retell it in his own words, being careful to give the facts in a logical order. If he feels he needs more information, tell him to ask the librarian for books on the topic. Guide him in selecting books he can read.

After he has written his report at home, ask him to read it aloud to be sure he has worded it well, then help him correct its spelling and punctuation. Do not change his wording—the report is his production. Writing the report was work enough; simply tell him how to spell words and punctuate it. Remember to praise him for a task well done.

Visiting the Public Library

Children who have reading disabilities usually also have weak vocabularies because they have not read enough to become familiar with many words. Reading is difficult for them, they seldom read for pleasure.

Encourage the child to search for information on topics that intrigue him. Form the habit of taking him to the library. On the way talk to him about the things he's interested in. If his interest is soccer, ask the librarian in the children's section where books on this sport are located. Tell her the child's reading level and ask her for assistance in locating easy-to-read books written for that level.

Select several books and quickly scan the first three pages of each one to make sure the child can read them with ease. The child should know ninety-seven words out of one hundred, otherwise the book is too hard. This does not include proper nouns (names). Have him apply for a library card and take home the two books he likes best.

At home, encourage him to read the books by himself. The child in the third grade should be encouraged to read at least one short book (sixty pages) each month. When he asks for help with an unknown word, tell him the word immediately; do not ask him to sound it. Being asked to stop and sound a word may interfere with his comprehension and make independent reading seem like work. Talk with him about what he has read, and laugh with him about events he feels are silly. Praise him lavishly when he finishes a book.

Teach him to look up items in encyclopedias, atlases, and almanacs. Encyclopedias have information about people, events, and other subjects. An atlas is a book of maps. The almanac has information about last year's events. If the child wants to know the names of last year's important soccer stars he should look in this year's almanac.

It is said that a person must have one thousand hours of reading practice to learn to read well. Library books are a great help in strengthening the child's reading skills and increasing his vocabulary.

Syllables

When the child has learned the phonics rules that I have given and can use them, he is ready to begin studying syllabication. I hope he has mastered these concepts by the time he is ready for the first third-grade reader.

Begin your lesson about syllables by telling the child that every syllable has at least one vowel, and that all syllables have vowel sounds.

The syllables that end with the letters **le** have the vowel sound of short **u** before the sound of the consonant **l**. When a word ends with **le** we usually add the consonant preceeding it to the **le** syllable. Say these words one at a time: table (ta ble), middle (mid dle), apple (ap ple), title (ti tle), circle (cir cle). Have the child tap the table to show the number of syllables in each word, then write the word dividing it into syllables. Call attention to the fact that the **le** syllable has the sound of **ul**.

Syllables that have **ck** before the **le** are exceptions to this rule. The **ck** is not divided; the ending syllable is **le**. Examples: Pickle (pick le), tickle (tick le), buckle (buck le). Have the child think of other words that end in **le**. Write them down and have him separate them into syllables.

Do not make your syllable lessons long. Be sure the child understands each rule or principle before you introduce a new one. Select common words, separate them into syllables, then decide which phonics rule applies to the vowel sound in each syllable as you pronounce it.

You might begin a lesson by tapping the table with your pencil as you say the word remember (re mem ber).

How many syllables are there in this word? (Three.) Write each syllable as you say it: "re-mem-ber." Notice there is a vowel in each syllable; each vowel follows a phonics rule you have learned.

re   The vowel at the end of a one-vowel word is long.
mem   The **e** is short because there is only one vowel followed by a consonant.
ber   The **er** is an r-controlled sound.

Tap another word, newspaper (news pa per). Three syllables. How many vowel sounds? Which rule do you use when sounding each vowel?

news   **Ew** is a diphthong.
pa   The **a** is long; it is at the end of a one-vowel syllable.
per   The **er** is an r-controlled sound.

Tap the word yesterday (yes ter day). Three syllables.

yes   The **e** is short; there is only one vowel followed by a consonant.
ter   The **er** is an r-controlled sound.
day   The **a** is long because it is the first vowel in a two-vowel syllable.

Separate these words into syllables and have the child explain each syllable's vowel sound: ivy (i vy), rodeo (ro de o), equip (e quip), erase (e rase).

Have the child decide which rule is used in sounding each vowel in these words:

ivy (i vy)
    i   The **i** is long; it is the only letter in the first syllable.
    vy   The **y** has the long **e** sound because it ends a two-syllable word.
rodeo (ro de o)
    ro   The **o** is long; it ends a one-vowel syllable.
    de   The **e** is long; it is at the end of a one-vowel syllable.
    o   The **o** is long; it's the only letter in the last syllable.

equip (e quip)

e   The **e** is long; it's the only letter in the syllable.

quip The **u** here does not sound; it belongs to the **q**. The **i** is the only letter used as a vowel. Because the **i** is followed by a consonant, the **i** is short.

erase (e rase)

e   The **e** is long; it's the only letter in the first syllable.

rase   The **a** is long; it's the first vowel in a two-vowel syllable.

Say these words: tornado (tor na do); butterfly (but ter fly); snowball (snow ball); downtown (down town); dirty (dirt y). Write them, tap the number of syllables, then divide them into syllables as you write them again. Ask the child to help you decide which phonics rule is used for each syllable's sound.

Twice a week, spend about fifteen or twenty minutes studying syllables. When you introduce a vocabulary word that has two or three syllables, divide it according to the phonics rules the child has been taught. Say the word. Have him tell you the rule each syllable follows. If the word is easy to sound, have the child write the syllables as you say them slowly. Then, since he has learned to "unlock" that word by using phonics rules, include it in the sight-word group he is being asked to learn.

Very often the vowels in the middle syllables of three or four syllable words do not follow the phonics rules for pronouncing long and short vowels. A vowel may have the sound of the **a** in around, or an **i** may have its short sound. Be sure to call this to the child's attention when he is pronouncing long words. Examples: beautiful (beau ti ful), capital (cap i tal), American (A mer i can), astronomy (as tron o my), believable (be liev a ble), gravity (grav i ty).

Praise the child when he uses syllabication to pronounce a long word, and tell him he will soon be able to recognize and read many long words by sounding them this way.

Spelling Rules

1. Words. Words are made up of one or more syllables. Every syllable must have a vowel sound. A word has as many syllables as it has vowel sounds.

2. Short vowels.   If there is only one vowel in a syllable and it is followed by a consonant, that vowel is short. Examples: cat, men, fin, doll, rug, flash, such, crib, which, spring, hidden (hid den), unbend (un bend).

3. Long vowels.   If there are two or more vowels in a word or syllable, the first vowel is usually long and the second vowel is silent. Examples: sail, meat, like, hope, mule. Examples in syllables: teacher (teach er), sailor (sail or), unite (u nite), lonely (lone ly).

The vowel at the end of a one-vowel word is long. Examples: he, she, hi, why, my.

The vowel at the end of a one-vowel syllable is usually long in the first syllable of a word; it may also be long in other syllables. Examples: raven (ra ven), fever (fe ver), title (ti tle), hotel (ho tel), unit (u nit), erosion (e ro sion), rodeo (ro de o).

4. In the middle syllable of a longer word, a vowel may sound like the **a** in around. Because that vowel could be either an **a, e, i, o,** or **u,** the child will need to look in the dictionary to ascertain which vowel it should be.

5. Long vowels are frequently paired with certain silent vowels. Some vowels are long because of a consonant pattern. Knowing these combinations makes spelling easier.

> Long **a**   **ai**—nail, sail, wait
> **ay**—may, say, way
> (The **ay** is at the end of a word.)
> **a-e**—game, cake, safe
> Long **e**   **ea**—sea, leaf, seat
> **ee**—tree, meet, feed
> **ie** or **ei**—believe, receive
> (Have the child memorize this rhyme: **I** before **e,** except after **c,** or when sounded like **a,** as in neighbor and weigh.)
> Long **i**   **i-e**—line, smile, fire
> **ie**—pie, tie, die
> (The **ie** is used at the end of words.)
> **ild**—wild, child, mild
> **ight**—light, fight, bright
> **ind**—find, kind, blind

Long o   oa—coat, road, soap
           ow—grow, snow, low
           (The **ow** is used at the end of words.)
           o-e—joke, hole, note
           old—cold, hold, fold
Long u   u-e—use, huge, cute
           The long **u** sound is also spelled:
           oo—moon, boot, room
           ew—new, few, blew

6. The r-controlled vowels.   There is no easy rule for spelling words that contain the r-controlled vowels **er**, **ir**, **ur**, **ear**, and **or** when they sound like the **r** in her. Dictionaries use a schwa when writing their sounds. The schwa looks like an upside-down **e**. Their sounds are written alike: her (hər), shirt (shərt), burn (bərn), earn (ərn), sailor (sāl ər). To know which vowel is used the child must learn to spell the word. Examples: girl, clerk, turn, birth, heard, skirt, fern, hurt, early.

Some words that name persons with special occupations end with **or**, but most of them end with **er**. Examples: sailor, doctor, inventor, surveyor, navigator, explorer, lawyer, farmer, teacher, carpenter, printer, reporter, drummer, juggler.

If two things are being compared, the word ends with **er**. Examples: bigger, taller, sweeter, prettier, harder, colder.

7. The r-controlled vowel **ar** often has the sound you hear in these words: arm, hard, jar, star, car, barn, mark, dark, part, far, garden.

The r-controlled vowel **or** often has the sound you hear in these words: for, horn, story, horse, born, north, forgot, cork, forth.

Mix these r-controlled words as you say them one at a time, pausing in between each word so the child can tell you which r-controlled vowel is in the word.

Ask the child to write the words as you pronounce the mixed lists using each word in a short sentence. Say, "Far, he lived far away, far. For, I baked it for you, for."

8. Consonant r-blends.   Children often find it difficult to decide whether the word should have a vowel before or after the **r**. Ask the child to say the word slowly, listening for the sound of a vowel. If he hears a vowel after the **r** sound, he should write the vowel after the blends. Exam-

ples: fright, drop, crack, struck, print, scrape, spring, treat, strong, grill, brand, shrug, tramp.

If the child does not hear a vowel after the **r** sound, the vowel is an r-controlled vowel, and it is before the **r**. Examples: girl, perch, curb, dirt, turn, clerk, shirt, burn, fern, chirp, twirl, herd, first.

Remember, every syllable must have at least one vowel; all words contain vowels.

9. The consonant **w** and the consonant digraph **wh**.   Some children have difficulty distinguishing between the sounds of **w** and **wh**.

Have the child look into a mirror as he says the following words: will, well, work, witch, watch. Then have him say these words: while, where, which, why, what. Ask him if he noticed that he blew air out slightly as he said the **wh**. The dictionary pronunciation key marks the sound of this digraph **hw**. Listen, blending these two sounds together, as you say where, which, why, and what.

Pronounce these words one at a time, having him tell you whether the word began with **w** or **wh**: wind, when, were, well, which, witch, we'll, wheel, wheat, weak, with, whiz, whether, weather.

Have the child write each word as you pronounce it and use it in a short sentence. Be patient. It may be necessary for you to repeat this lesson several times, but eventually he will learn to distinguish the sounds. Praise him for his accomplishment.

10. The soft and hard sounds of **c**.   Soft **c** has the sound of **s** as in city. **C** only has the soft sound when it is followed by one of the three vowels, **e**, **i**, or **y**. The vowel must be the first letter after the **c**. Examples: cedar, celery, cell, cent, city, circle, circus, citizen, cyclone, cycle, cymbal.

If the **c** is followed by any other letter (with the exception of the digraph **ch**, as in church), the **c** has the hard sound of **k**. Examples: cake, catch, choir, clap, class, coat, count, cross, cut, curl.

Whenever you spell the hard sound of **c** followed by an **e**, **i**, or **y**, you must begin the word with a **k**. Examples: keep, keg, key, kick, kind, kite, kitten.

11. The soft and hard sounds of **g**.   Soft **g** has the sound of **j** as in jar. **G** usually has the soft sound of **j** when it is followed by an **e**, **i**, or **y**. The vowel must be the first letter after the **g**. Examples: germ, gem, gentle, general, giant, ginger, gym, Gypsy.

There are exceptions to this rule: get, gear, gift, give, given, giggle, gill.

If the **g** is followed by any other letter it has the hard sound, with the exception of **gh**, as in rough or cough. **G** also has the hard sound when it ends a word. Examples: flag, game, glad, good, grade, gum, jog.

12. Adding the suffixes **s**, **es**, and **ed**.   Tapping the plural of a word to ascertain how many syllables the word has is an easy way to find out whether to add **s** or **es**.

If you add an **s** to the word bush and then try to say "bushs," you cannot seem to make the word sound different. Now change bush to a two-syllable word by adding an **es**, bushes. It is easy to tell that this is the correct spelling.

If a word ends with a vowel followed by **y**, just add **s**, **ed**, or **ing**. Examples: tray, trays; key, keyed; say, saying.

If an **es** is added to key, making it "keyes," it is easy to hear that this is wrong. Add only an **s** and you have the one-syllable word keys.

Ask the child to tap the table to find the number of syllables in the plurals of these words and to tell you whether they end in an **s** or **es**: desk, wish, boy, bird, bunch, fox, dog, girl, lunch, guess, cuff, screw, day, disk, pig, dress, dish.

If a word ends with a consonant followed by **y**, change the **y** to **i** before adding **es**, **ed**, or **est**. Examples: baby, babies; fly, flies; lady, ladies; candy, candies; bunny, bunnies; cry, cries, cried; try, tries, tried; pretty, prettier, prettiest; funny, funnier, funniest.

Tell the child that we never put three of the vowels **a**, **e**, **i**, **o**, or **u** together in a word. Play would look very strange if we changed its **y** to an **i** and spelled it "plaies." Also, we wouldn't add an **es** to play changing it to a two-syllable word, "playes," instead of plays.

13. When adding **ed**, **er**, **est**, or **ing** to words that end in a silent **e**, drop the silent **e**. Examples: chase, chased; name, named; bake, baked; wide, wider; nice, nicer; late, later; close, closest; white, whitest; little, littlest; bake, baking; ride, riding; save, saving.

14. If a short vowel word ends in only one consonant, double the consonant before adding a suffix that begins with a vowel. Examples: hop, hopped; ship, shipped; quit, quitting; run, running.

You do not double the letter at the end of short vowel words that end in two consonants. Examples: hush, hushed; jump, jumped; patch, patched; help, helped; lick, licking; kiss, kissing.

15. The digraph **ch** has two sounds—**ch** as in church and the sound of **k** as in school. When the digraph **ch** as in church begins a word, it is followed by a vowel.

Examples: chat, cheer, chick, chop, chum.

At the end of a word the **ch** follows either a vowel or a consonant. Examples: lunch, bench, match, which, teach, switch.

When the **ch** has the **k** sound, it may be followed by either a vowel or a consonant. Examples: choir, Christmas, chord, chorus.

16. The apostrophe shows ownership. It is used only if the name of the thing owned follows the name of its owner. The possessive form of a singular noun, its name, is formed by adding an apostrophe and an **s** to the noun. Notice the apostrophe in this sentence: Hang the boy's coat in the closet. Examples: teacher's desk, Dad's car, dog's bone, Tom's bat, Mary's dress.

To form the possessive form of a plural noun, first write the plural noun, then do one of two things:

If the plural form ends in an **s**, add an apostrophe after the **s**. Examples: two boys, two boys' coats; three girls, three girls' dresses; two babies, two babies' toys; the wolves, the wolves' den.

If the plural does not end in an **s**, add an apostrophe and an **s**. Examples: three men, three men's cars; the children, the children's party; the mice, the mice's cage; the women, the women's club.

17. Have the child learn to spell these common suffixes and word endings:

_le as in people (peo ple), apple (ap ple), bicycle (bi cy cle), rattle (rat tle). Notice that the last syllable of these words is formed by a consonant plus **le**.

ment as in statement (state ment), movement (move ment), experiment (ex per i ment), payment (pay ment)

ful as in bashful (bash ful), wonderful (won der ful), thankful (thank ful), careful (care ful)

ing as in loving (lov ing), fighting (fight ing), kicking (kick ing), saying (say ing)

ness as in kindness (kind ness), illness (ill ness), hardness (hard ness), sickness (sick ness)

less as in helpless (help less), shapeless (shape less), useless (use less), blameless (blame less)

tion as in mention (men tion), attention (at ten tion), condition (con di tion), vacation (va ca tion)

ous as in curious (cu ri ous), famous (fa mous), nervous (ner vous), serious (se ri ous)

ture as in picture (pic ture), adventure (ad ven ture), furniture (fur ni ture), nature (na ture)

There are lists of words ending with suffixes in Part Three of this book. After the child has memorized the spellings of the suffixes, pronounce them ten at a time. Use them, not for spelling words to be memorized, but for words to be spelled by using spelling rules.

There are other endings the child in the third grade should learn to recognize and in later grades learn to spell: **cious** as in delicious (de li cious), **tious** as in ambitious (am bi tious), **ence** as in conference (con fer ence), **ance** as in appearance (ap pear ance), **cial** as in special (spe cial), and **tial** as in initial (i ni tial).

Do not discourage the child by insisting he learn to spell long lists of words. Introduce endings and suffixes when they occur in reading vocabulary. Teach him to recognize and pronounce endings, and to spell them a few at a time.

When a child sets out to write a story, he need not stop to look up words he does not know how to spell. He should just write them the way he thinks they may be spelled. Stopping to look up the words at that time will destroy the continuity of his thoughts and may ruin his story. However, as soon as the story is completed, he should look up the spellings of the words he is not sure of.

It is important to teach the child how to look up the spellings of words in the dictionary. Even though a dyslexic thinks he has mastered the spellings of words, he may forget them quickly. The dictionary should become a very special friend.

Rules for Dividing Words Into Syllables

There are some helpful rules for dividing words into syllables and pronouncing them that should be taught to the child when he is reading at the third-grade level.

1. A compound word is a word made up of two or more short words. It is divided between the short words. Examples: cupcake (cup cake), mailbox (mail box), someone (some one), myself (my self), football (foot ball), airport (air port), outside (out side), birthday (birth day).

2. When a two-syllable word has two consonants after a vowel, it is usually divided between the two consonants. Because every syllable of a word has a vowel, you could write this rule: vowel, consonant, divide, consonant, vowel, or VC/CV. In the word doctor, o is the first vowel. It is followed by two consonants, c and t. Divide between c and t this way: doc tor. Examples: dentist (den tist), cartoon (car toon), counter (coun ter), goblin (gob lin), chipmunk (chip munk), window (win dow), fancy (fan cy), sentence (sen tence), umbrella (um brel la).

All consonant blends (**str, pr, sp, cl, sw, sk, nk, lt, ng**, and so forth) are treated as if they were one consonant. Examples: complete (com plete), increase (in crease), kingdom (king dom), angry (an gry), construct (con struct), inflate (in flate), transfer (trans fer).

All consonant digraphs (**ch, ph, ck, sh, th, wh**) are treated as if they were one consonant. Examples: anchor (an chor), merchant (mer chant), farther (far ther), orphan (or phan), mushroom (mush room).

3. When a two-syllable word has one consonant between two vowels, it is usually divided in front of the consonant and the first vowel is long. You could write this rule: vowel, divide, consonant, vowel, or V/CV. Examples: secret (se cret), pupil (pu pil), label (la bel), spider (spi der), favor (fa vor), music (mu sic), hotel (ho tel), open (o pen).

4. If a two-syllable word that has only one consonant between two vowels is divided after the consonant, the first vowel is short. You could write this rule: vowel, consonant, divide, vowel, or VC/V. Examples: wagon (wag on), seven (sev en), visit (vis it), robin (rob in), punish (pun ish), shadow (shad ow), rocket (rock et), cabin (cab in), dragon (drag on), camel (cam el).

There are many words that have only one consonant between two vowels. Teach the child that if he sounds a word using the V/CV rule and the "word" he gets doesn't fit into the sentence he is reading, he must then sound it using the VC/V rule.

5. A suffix is one or more letters added to the end of a word. If the suffix has a vowel sound, it is a syllable.

The suffixes in these words are syllables; they have vowel sounds: careful (care ful), gladly (glad ly), newer (new er), greenest (green est), folded (fold ed), bushes (bush es), playing (play ing), painted (paint ed).

The suffixes in these words do not have vowel sounds, therefore they are not syllables: plates, tried, washed, dropped, seeds.

6. Do not use the V/CV rule when dividing words from which you have dropped the **e** at the end of a root word and then added the suffix. (A root word is a word from which other words may be made by adding a prefix or suffix. In the word discolored, the root word is color.)

When you separate these words into syllables, you must remember you have dropped the **e** from the root word. If you are writing the word fading, you drop the **e** from fade. You write **fad**, then add the suffix **ing** to make fading. Then you separate fading into two syllables: fad ing.

You could write this rule: vowel, consonant, divide, suffix, or VC/S. Use this rule only for separating a word from which you have dropped the final **e** from the root word. The first vowel in these words is long. Example: hope, hoping, (hop ing); tape, taping, (tap ing); file, filing, (fil ing); ride, riding, (rid ing); fade, faded, (fad ed); hike, hiker, (hik er).

7. When you add a suffix to a word whose first vowel is short, if it has only one consonant after the short vowel you double that consonant. You usually follow the VC/CV rule when you separate such a word into syllables. Examples: hop, hopping, (hop ping); tap, tapping, (tap ping); big, bigger, (big ger); flip, flipper, (flip per); run, running, (run ning).

8. Many suffixes that have vowels lose their vowel sound when they are added to words. Although these words end with suffixes, they cannot be divided after the root words. Examples: filled, played, puffed, parked, boxed, aimed, called, leaped, kissed, crawled.

9. A prefix is a letter or group of letters added to the beginning of a word. Each prefix has a meaning of its own. Prefixes change the meanings of the words to which they are added.

The prefix **un** means "not," or "the opposite of." Unkind means "not kind;" uncover means "the opposite of cover." The prefix **pre** means "before." Prehistoric means "before history was written."

Because all prefixes contain vowels, they are syllables added to the beginnings of words. Have the child say these words, and talk about how the prefix changes the meaning of each word: untie (un tie), defrost (de frost), rebuild (re build), distrust (dis trust), mistreat (mis treat), alike (a like), exhale (ex hale), inhale (in hale).

10. If the first or last syllable of a word has only one vowel, and that vowel is at the syllable's end, the vowel is usually long. Examples: even (e ven), giant (gi ant), poem (po em), create (cre ate), rodeo (ro de o), radio (ra di o).

An exception to this rule is when the first syllable is an **a**. Then **a** usually has the sound of the **a** in around. Examples: ahead (a head), alone (a lone), about (a bout), alive (a live).

You will find sheets for practice in spelling and dividing words into syllables in Part Three of this book.

Using the Dictionary in the Third Grade

Most third-, fourth-, and fifth-grade readers have glossaries. Learning to use the glossary will teach the child dictionary skills. The glossary contains a pronunciation key, lists in alphabetical order the difficult words in the book, divides them into syllables, tells how to pronounce them, and gives their meanings. When the child doesn't know the meaning of a word, teach him to look it up in the glossary. If the word is not in the glossary, he should look it up in the dictionary.

He should be taught that the dictionary gives the entry word, then its pronunciation, followed by the way it is used and its meaning.

The dictionary indicates how words are used with abbreviations: **n**, **vb**, **adj**, and **adv**. Teach the child what these abbreviations stand for.

n   (noun): a name of a person, place, or thing
vb   (verb): an action word
adj   (adjective): a word that describes or limits
adv   (adverb): a word that tells how, when, where, or why

Ask the child to look up the word saw. He will find these entries:

saw/'sȯ/n 1 : a tool or instrument with a tooth-edged blade for cutting material 2 : a machine that operates a toothed blade
      saw vb : to cut or shape with a saw

Many words have more than one meaning. Suppose the child is looking for the meaning of down in this sentence: The bodies of young birds were covered with down. His dictionary has down listed seven times as an entry word. Two of the entry words have several meanings. If he knows that he is looking for the meaning of a noun, he will be able to find the correct one quickly. There are only three short entries listed as nouns. The child will find this shortcut interesting; call it to his attention.

Pronunciation Keys

Dictionaries and glossaries have pronunciation keys at the bottoms of their pages. The key gives the pronunciation symbols used for the vowel sounds in that book. Teach the child how to use the pronunciation key.

In most pronunciation keys the vowels **a**, **e**, and **i** are short if they are not marked. Examples: hat, set, and kit.

Short **o**'s are marked with various symbols. Check the pronunciation key in the book you are using for their markings.

The short vowel **u** is marked with the symbol, ə. This is the schwa, which looks like an upside-down **e**. Examples: tug (təg), must (məst), but (bət).

If the **u** has the vowel sound you hear in blue, the **u** is marked with the symbol, **ü**. Examples: blue (blü), glue (glü), due (dü), rule (rül), fruit (früt).

If the **u** has the vowel sound you hear in good and put, it is marked with the symbol, **u̇**. Examples: put (pu̇t), bush (bu̇sh), push (pu̇sh), hood (hu̇d), book (bu̇k).

Very often the vowels in the middle of a three- or four-syllable word have the schwa sound, or the **i** has its short sound. Examples: serious (se ri ous), position (po si tion), television (tel e vi sion), victorious (vic to ri ous), accident (ac ci dent), president (pres i dent), musical (mu si cal), furniture (fur ni ture), difficult (dif fi cult), medicine (med i cine).

Knowing this will help the child when he is learning to pronounce longer words.

Accents

When we pronounce a word of more than one syllable, we usually give one of the syllables more importance than the others. We do this by saying the more important syllable with more force or stress. The syllable we stress is said to be accented.

Most dictionaries now mark accented syllables with a tiny accent symbol, or a tiny straight line, set above the line at the beginning of the syllable that is accented, like this: behold (be 'hold), zero ('ze ro).

Some dictionaries place an accent mark in the upper half of the space after the accented syllable. For example: behold (be hold'), zero (ze' ro). If the child's dictionary uses this accent mark, teach him its meaning.

Ask the child to place his thumb under his chin. Tell him to say the word candy. Which syllable seems to be the most important? Can, it is the accented syllable ('can dy). Try these words: cheerful ('cheer ful), explode (ex 'plode), parade (pa 'rade), happy ('hap py), rubber ('rub ber), protect (pro 'tect), hurry ('hur ry), pretend (pre 'tend).

In two-syllable words, the accent is usually on the first syllable unless the last syllable has two vowels, or if the first syllable is a prefix. Examples: baby ('ba by); angel ('an gel); cabin ('cab in); suppose (sup 'pose); machine (ma 'chine); advise (ad 'vise); recall (re 'call); depart (de 'part); misspell (mis 'spell).

Compound words are usually accented on the first syllable. Examples: topcoat ('top coat); bedtime ('bed time); sportsman ('sports man).

Suffixes as well as prefixes are not stressed; they are not accented syllables. Examples: tanker ('tank er); calling ('call ing); bushes ('bush es); depend (de 'pend); remark (re 'mark); indent (in 'dent).

Often when a child has correctly sounded all the syllables of a word, he is still unable to say it because he has misplaced the accent. Say the word several times for him, stressing different syllables until he recognizes the word. This will teach him how to stress accented syllables and also help him realize the importance of accents.

The Schwa

One of the commonest vowel sounds in the English language is the schwa. In the dictionary the symbol for the schwa sound is ə. It looks like an upside-down e.

The vowel sound may be spelled with **a, e, i, o, u,** or **oo**. It is the sound we give the **a** in about (ə bout), **e** in kitten (kit tən), the **i** in pupil (pu pəl), the **o** in son (sən), the **u** in bug (bəg), and the **oo** in blood (bləd).

Often in words of more than one syllable, the vowel in the unstressed syllable (the syllable that is not accented) has the schwa sound. Because we cannot tell which vowel the schwa sound in a word stands for, we have to work harder to learn to spell many words. Examples: open, lemon, medal, rabbit, sharpen, magnet, April, season, animal.

Teach the child how to find the correct spelling of a word that contains a schwa. Let's suppose he does not know how to spell touch. The word sounds like it is spelled t-u-c-h. He looks for "tuch" and cannot find it. Then he knows that the vowel in touch is a schwa. He also knows that schwas are always vowels; the vowels are **a, e, i, o,** and **u.** He looks in the dictionary, again using the vowel he thinks might be the schwa. When he finds touch with its definition, he knows he has its correct spelling.

Dictionaries also use the schwa symbol to mark the r-controlled sound we hear in her (hər), bird (bərd), and hurt (hərt).

Reading Speed

We read with our minds. Our eyes are the "camera" that sends the pictures of the written symbols to the brain. The brain interprets the meaning of the symbols.

If you watch a child read, you will note that his eyes move along the line, stopping here and there. The stops the eyes make are called fixations. Most reading time is spent on fixations. At each fixation the eyes send a picture of the symbols it sees to the mind, where they are turned into meaning.

If the child's eyes pause to recognize each word, he will get very little meaning from his reading, and his reading speed will be very slow. His comprehension will be poor because his mind is receiving thought in small bits.

After a beginner reads a page orally word-for-word, the parent should read the page to him and then ask the child to reread it, making it sound like he is talking. This will help the child to learn to group the words he is reading into phrases. Because his eyes make fewer fixations, his reading will become more fluent, he will gain speed, and his comprehension will improve.

If he finds phrasing difficult, read a page to him as you move your pencil above the line, pausing at the end of each phrase, then have the child read the same page. Have him practice reading additional pages as you move your pencil above the line to indicate the phrasing. Watch carefully to be sure he does not form the habit of rereading words. Pausing to reread words soon becomes a habit and interferes with developing speed.

As soon as the child is able to read well orally in phrases, ask him to read paragraphs silently. At first he will probably whisper the words. Let him do this for a week or two, then tell him his eyes can read words faster than his lips can whisper them; if he does not say the words, his reading speed will increase. The mind is like a computer—it can give thought to word symbols at an amazing rate.

Talk to the child about reading speed. Call his attention to the fact that he can read a book for pleasure very fast, scanning pages occasionally, but when he reads his science lesson he will need to decrease his speed and stop now and then to think about what he has just read. He can read faster about interesting, familiar things than about topics that are new to him. If he reads too slowly his thoughts may wander, and he may even daydream. Forcing himself to read faster will help him pay attention.

The older child should make a definite effort to increase his reading speed. He can do this by forcing himself to read faster as he groups words together in longer and longer phrases. He should not whisper or reread words or move parts of his body in rhythm to his reading.

He may enjoy using a stop watch, timing his reading of pages of similar difficulty. Tell him to record the time it takes for him to read each of three to five pages. After recording the reading time for a page, he must stop to ask himself what he has just read. If he is able to stop saying the words to himself subconsciously as he reads, he will gain much speed. Very rapid readers are able to do this. Remember, speed and comprehension must always go forward together.

Pictures, Charts, and Word Lists You Can Use to Teach Your Child to Read

Part Three contains materials for use in tutoring your child. The pictures, charts, and word lists should be photocopied and enlarged.

The enlarged pictures should be cut apart and used for teaching the consonant and digraph sounds.

The Most Used Words lists should be enlarged to the size of the words in the child's primer. Two sets of these words are needed. Cut apart the words on one set and use them to make flash cards. Save the other set for spelling lessons.

The word charts, pages 113–30, are for practice in recognizing and pronouncing phonics sounds. Lay a paper strip one inch wide and nine inches long beneath the line and have the child read the words from left to right as you slide the strip down the page. Save these sheets in a folder for future reference and review.

The syllable sheets, pages 134–49, are for practice in dividing words into syllables and learning how to spell them. Before you use these sheets, have several photocopies made—you will probably need them for additional practice.

INITIAL CONSONANT PICTURES

These pictures are for use in teaching the initial consonant sounds. Cut them apart and put each letter's pictures in a separate envelope.

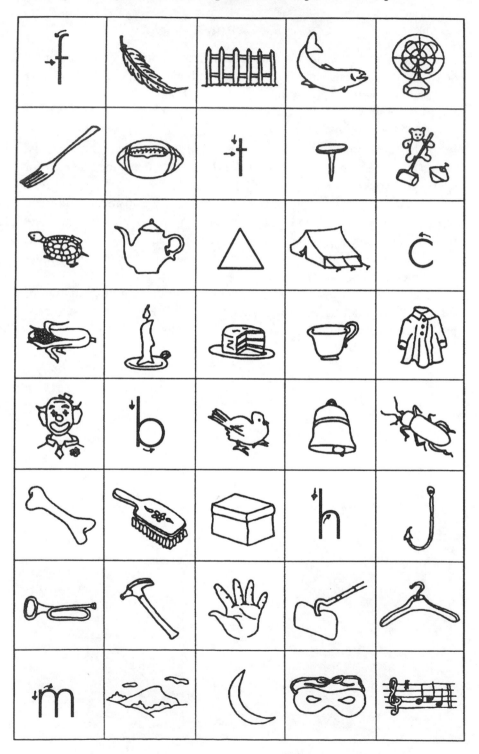

Initial Consonant Pictures

INITIAL CONSONANT AND DIGRAPH PICTURES

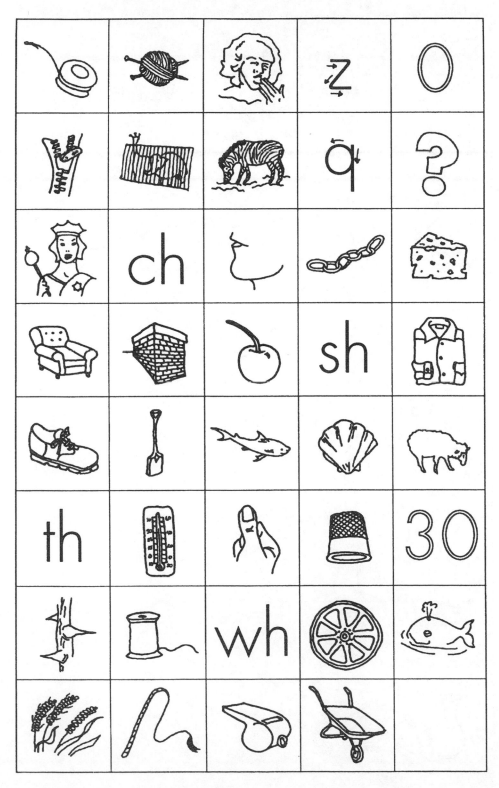

VOWEL CHARTS

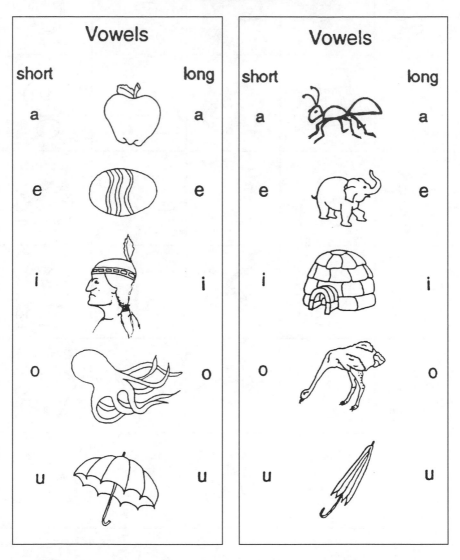

MANUSCRIPT ALPHABET

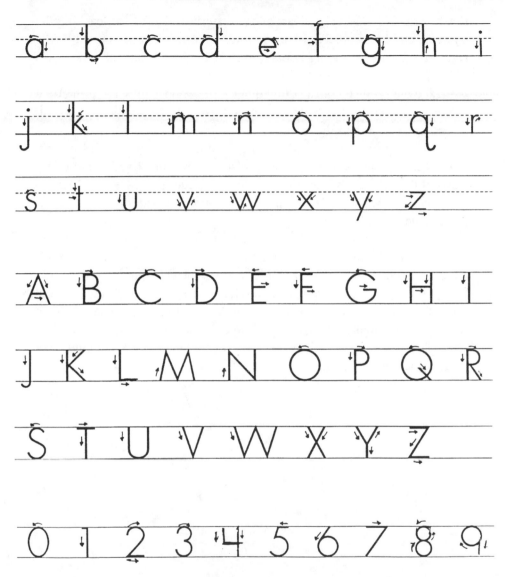

FLASH CARDS

Flash cards are a necessary part of the materials needed for teaching the dyslexic child to read. The printed words on each card set should be the right size for their reading book's level. It is not difficult to make flash cards.

Take the book's word list to a quick-print shop. Show the printer the words on a page of the basic reader and ask him to photocopy the list, enlarging its words to that size.

You can purchase the cards you need at the print shop. Ask for cards 2 ¼″ × 2 ¹³⁄₁₆″ cut from 67-pound cardstock. Because one hundred fifty cards of this size can be cut from ten sheets of letter size (8 ½″ × 11″) cardstock without waste, it is usually best to purchase one hundred fifty or three hundred cards at a time.

Cut the words apart and attach each one to the center of a card with Scotch tape. On the back of each card write the number of the book's page upon which that word first occurs. Stack the cards in numerical order and put a rubber band around them. Hold the stack firmly together and color the stack's lower edge with a marker. Coloring each set's edge a different color makes it easy to replace cards taken out for review. Save your flash card sets—you may need to use them again, or you might want to give them to a friend.

Most Used Words

A	B	C	D	E
said	big	away	at	work
play	here	in	ran	us
see	will	was	fast	ten
come	she	make	cold	so
red	it	going	had	his
you	yes	help	one	all
little	down	out	her	find
the	on	after	they	came
look	stop	with	walk	how
he	like	under	did	long
to	blue	into	if	too
up	not	we	three	again
me	want	green	put	new
run	of	some	round	sit
jump	but	two	over	went
and	who	from	no	do
go	good	what	your	gave
saw	him	fly	made	could
for	around	them	when	many
have	call	now	give	that
are	yellow	soon	funny	hot
is	can	an	as	am
get	this	be	its	upon
my	by	were	found	those
eat	old	take	tell	let

Most Used Words

F	G	H	I	J
live	which	every	well	build
black	warm	should	thank	four
where	about	six	laugh	drive
ride	there	only	own	sound
know	keep	these	second	each
been	very	because	both	better
has	pick	clean	listen	caught
got	does	try	use	white
think	our	hurt	seven	nothing
once	read	write	just	third
bring	before	eight	begin	sure
say	must	far	left	build
may	pretty	pull	thought	start
ate	talk	buy	even	enough
open	hold	sleep	ready	carry
them	never	best	busy	together
ask	light	goes	cut	whole
much	brown	draw	always	myself
show	shall	their	five	guess
done	would	learn	wrong	bought
or	please	small	drink	through
wish	first	kind	right	believe
off	today	full	count	almost
grow	sing	any	beside	leave
fall	why	wash	paid	often

SHORT VOWELS

Short a

nap	lad	jam	way	can
bag	man	lap	sad	pat
can	cat	gas	map	tag
dad	van	bat	pass	ran

Short i

win	hit	mill	big	zip
fib	did	fin	hill	lid
sip	wig	rib	mitt	him
bill	hip	pin	dig	miss

Short o

fog	job	mop	not	moss
doll	log	got	pod	boss
top	lot	nod	mob	jog
dot	rob	cop	toss	sob

Short u

tub	gum	mud	fuzz	gun
puff	rug	fun	nut	pup
hum	bud	bug	muss	dull
bus	mug	buzz	hug	bun

Short e

bell	net	red	den	web
set	men	jet	beg	fed
peg	fell	wet	egg	pet
tell	less	bed	hen	yes

Please note: The dictionary does not mark short vowel sounds.

SHORT VOWEL MIX-UPS

Short a, i, o

tap	miss	pop	bill	dot
hip	van	doll	pan	mill
log	fin	wag	boss	gas
jam	nod	did	lap	win
wig	jog	sad	fog	pass

Short e, i, u

pet	big	rug	yes	nut
bus	gum	men	hill	fib
tip	web	pup	dig	bell
hum	him	net	dull	fuzz
fig	egg	mug	fed	lip

Short a, e, o

pat	red	job	den	map
peg	cat	God	tan	got
bag	fog	jet	moss	fell
sob	bed	dad	not	rap
wet	jog	set	hen	top

Short a, e, i, o, u

less	hug	rib	boss	nap
pod	zip	beg	puff	fan
nip	well	cop	lad	tub
mud	pin	fan	bet	nod
man	buzz	hit	rob	bed

LONG VOWELS

Long **a** (Dictionaries mark this vowel ā)

gain	say	trail	may	hair
safe	fair	chain	aim	pray
fail	care	stay	rain	quail
plane	mail	paint	fake	snail

Long **e** (Dictionaries mark this vowel ē.)

sweet	leaf	need	peach	she
fear	feet	teach	dear	free
key	wc	sleep	feel	clear
freeze	ear	cheat	squeal	seat

Long **i** (Dictionaries mark this vowel ī.)

pine	mile	kite	bride	smile
light	prize	line	quite	wide
size	time	ripe	shine	fight
wife	vine	fight	hive	wire

Long **o** (Dictionaries mark this vowel ō.)

coat	joke	bone	hope	grow
hoe	stove	note	boat	froze
snow	goat	woke	slow	road
pole	vote	flow	float	cone

Long **u** (Dictionaries mark this vowel ü.)

cure	use	mule	cube	pure
fuse	cute	muse	huge	mute
yule	fume	duke	June	brute
tune	lute	tube	rule	Luke

LONG VOWEL MIX-UPS

Long **a, i, o**

mail	joke	quite	snow	prize
shine	pray	froze	smile	cone
stove	right	safe	chain	size
hair	grow	wife	stay	hoe
wire	care	goat	kite	quail

Long **e, i, u**

wide	cute	freeze	pure	key
leaf	hive	cube	line	huge
tune	light	might	she	duke
teach	sweet	rule	seat	bride
fuse	squeal	vine	cheat	pine

Long **a, e, o**

dear	coat	rain	cheat	slow
aim	throw	peach	bone	gain
woke	trail	plane	road	fear
sleep	boat	fair	clear	note
may	need	rode	hail	leaf

Long **a, e, i, o, u**

cube	feel	paint	bride	note
say	slow	mute	fine	meal
fake	cure	sight	goat	beach
mile	snail	road	she	tube
key	hope	tray	use	mile

SHORT VOWELS CHANGED TO LONG

Read these words in pairs. The first word in each column contains one short vowel. This vowel is short because it is followed by a consonant. The second word has two vowels—the first vowel is long, the second is silent.

mat	mate		pad	paid
fad	fade		red	read
back	bake		hid	hide
ran	rain		rod	rode
pal	pail		lad	laid
set	seat		tub	tube
led	lead		met	meet
ten	teen		cot	coat
fell	feel		bit	bite
wed	weed		rat	rate
kit	kite		bet	beat
fill	file		not	note
rip	ripe		Tim	time
did	died		sham	shame
win	wine		sell	seal
rob	robe		sop	soap
sock	soak		sack	sake
pop	pope		sit	site
rod	road		men	mean
got	goat		van	vane
tap	tape		twin	twine
bed	bead		rack	rake
mill	mile		net	neat
cod	code		rid	ride

Long and Short Vowel Mix-Ups

kit	kite	bat	bait	bake
Ben	bean	man	main	may
let	lead	cut	cute	cue
fat	fate	hid	hide	hi
ran	rain	met	meet	meat
cot	coat	rip	ripe	rice

mat	mate	got	goat	go
pad	paid	wed	weed	we
wag	wake	bit	bite	by
set	seat	sock	soak	so
van	vane	bed	bead	be
lad	laid	not	note	no

hug	huge	hue	bow	boat
sake	sack	hop	hope	hoe
seal	sell	sop	soap	sod
low	load	lot	tap	tape
twin	twine	road	rod	rode
quite	quit	fad	fade	file

beat	bet	beet	bell	bill
pain	pan	pal	pale	pail
team	ten	teen	tack	take
cat	Kate	kill	coke	core
rate	rat	wrote	rid	ride
sled	slide	slept	sleep	slick

CONSONANT DIGRAPHS

ch (Dictionaries indicate this sound ch.)

church	chin	chair	child	chick
chill	chain	check	chest	cheat
each	much	lunch	ouch	march

sh (Dictionaries indicate this sound sh.)

ship	shall	shirt	shut	shoe
sheep	shine	shot	shout	shell
rush	dash	fish	wash	wish

th (Dictionaries indicate this sound th.)

them	that	there	these	this
those	though	then	they	than
bathe	paths	clothe	with	booths

th (Dictionaries indicate this sound th.)

thin	throat	think	thief	thumb
thread	thorn	thaw	thought	thank
bath	width	youth	health	south

wh (Dictionaries indicate this sound hw.)

what	where	whirl	wheat	when
which	white	whine	while	wheel
whale	wheeze	whiff	whiz	whip

Consonant Digraph Mix-Ups

ch, sh

chill	sheet	lunch	chain	shine
ship	fish	chin	shell	chick
reach	check	shout	chair	shirt
sheep	chip	march	wash	child

ch, wh

what	chest	where	cheat	wheel
child	white	church	whip	chick
whale	check	whiz	chain	why
such	when	teach	who	march

th (as in those), th (as in thin)

then	both	with	thick	these
they	cloth	there	them	moth
thief	than	this	north	thank
bath	bathe	tooth	path	math

ch, sh, wh

whale	chair	dish	while	chin
shot	wheeze	cheese	push	where
chest	shoot	which	chain	fresh
cash	porch	mush	crash	lunch

ch, th, wh

church	white	bath	branch	when
whip	bench	cloth	why	thin
catch	wheel	inch	throw	what
with	which	path	pinch	broth

INITIAL CONSONANT BLENDS

bl, cl, fl, gl, pl

clip	flash	glass	plate	blink
glow	black	play	flip	clear
flag	plot	blend	club	glide
class	flock	glad	blue	plant
globe	clap	bloom	plum	fly

sl, sm, sn, sp, spl

snake	space	smack	sled	splash
smoke	splint	spill	snap	slide
split	snail	slip	smell	spark
sleep	speak	sneak	splash	smash
spell	smile	split	slick	snow

sc, sk, st, sw, tw

stoop	scab	twig	skill	sweet
swell	twin	stone	scar	skim
scare	tweet	skate	swing	still
twin	skid	stink	scarf	switch
skip	stub	swim	twice	scale

Initial Consonant Blend Mix-Up

flash	blend	spill	snap	club
store	snow	plant	twin	sled
scarf	fly	speak	bloom	stove
slick	twig	sweep	smile	plum
swift	globe	flesh	skip	switch

INITIAL CONSONANT BLENDS

br, cr, dr, fr, gr

free	brush	crab	grate	dry
crop	drop	blue	fresh	grill
drive	green	frame	brain	crate
brag	crash	fret	drink	grip
gray	drum	crawl	brown	frog

scr, spr, str, tr, squ

spread	string	trot	scream	squeal
strap	trunk	screw	spring	square
scrub	strange	spray	try	squash
scrape	true	sprain	stray	squint
streak	scrap	tray	sprout	squaw

Initial Consonant Blend Mix-Up

frank	trim	drug	stream	creak
grape	breed	spray	scrub	tribe
strain	crib	fresh	bright	square
cross	screw	drip	trick	squeak
scrape	grand	drill	stroke	bright

Initial Consonant Blend Mix-Up

strike	snip	flag	ground	sprout
swell	crisp	smack	snap	plate
glass	smell	droop	drip	frown
skill	scrape	grain	treat	cry
splash	spy	blew	scare	square

CONSONANT BLEND ENDINGS

ft, ld, mp, ng, nk

song	jump	blink	bold	lift
gang	drift	fold	cramp	pink
hold	crank	shrimp	gift	sting
camp	held	left	frank	thing
soft	tramp	drink	strong	mold

lt, nd, nt, sp, st

brand	crust	felt	crisp	print
mist	hint	grand	gasp	belt
lisp	grunt	mind	bolt	pest
ground	fault	mint	must	rasp
melt	blond	vest	harp	hunt

ct, lk, lp, pt, sk

kept	silk	help	desk	facts
yelp	risk	wept	walk	helps
fact	chalk	kelp	slept	disk
gulp	crept	dusk	act	milk
desks	acts	talks	gulps	prompt

Consonant Blend Endings Mix-Up

lungs	tank	went	bold	kept
best	dust	loft	runt	quilt
hound	fact	stunt	long	crust
junk	dump	trust	molt	front
help	jolt	walk	crisp	risk

Diphthongs

au, aw (Dictionaries indicate this sound as ȯ.)

cause	yawn	fault	crawl	launch
claw	hawk	Paul	lawn	flaw
taught	pause	law	dawn	taunt
draw	shawl	haul	haunt	thaw

ew, oo as in moon (Dictionaries indicate this sound ü.)

grew	bloom	zoom	stew	pool
tooth	blew	flew	cool	smooth
moon	crew	chew	boot	spoon
few	drew	broom	dew	brew

oi, oy (Dictionaries indicate this sound ȯi.)

oil	noise	moist	spoil	joy
voice	boy	soil	hoist	coil
toy	broil	Roy	point	boil
coin	join	toys	joint	boys

oo as in book (Dictionaries indicate this sound u̇.)

look	stood	took	shook	good
soot	crook	hood	book	cook
foot	wood	brook	stood	wool
poor	hook	wool	nook	foot

ou, ow (Dictionaries indicate this sound au̇.)

scout	cloud	gown	ground	round
loud	how	our	crown	frown
howl	hound	south	chow	pout
brown	down	flour	clown	town

DIPHTHONG MIX-UPS

au, aw, ou, ow

jaw	sound	fawn	ouch	haul
taught	slaw	crawl	clown	snout
plow	chow	bound	cause	yawn
count	mouth	stout	sprawl	prowl
lawn	paw	caught	sprout	cloud

oi, oy, ew, oo

news	boy	voice	blew	cool
oil	crew	dew	point	chew
moist	toil	grew	zoom	joy
smooth	tooth	boil	boot	noise
join	few	coin	coil	drew

oo as in moon, oo as in book

booth	shook	hood	bloom	stood
wool	zoo	moon	boost	look
broom	took	stool	wood	smooth
cool	boot	crook	tooth	soon
book	pool	stoop	good	zoom

au, aw, ew, oi, oo, ou, ow, oy

joy	stood	soil	cause	join
draw	joint	caught	stool	lawn
bloom	zoo	spout	toys	spoil
wood	straw	grew	how	loud
flew	crowd	pause	wool	brew

R-Controlled Vowels

er, ir, ur (Dictionaries indicate this sound as ər.)

fern	curb	furs	whirl	stern
girl	perch	hurt	chirp	curve
turn	first	swerve	bird	herd
hers	curl	clerk	skirt	third
burn	firm	shirt	verse	nurse

ar (Dictionaries indicate this sound är.)

barn	war	lark	cart	march
part	dark	hard	scar	harm
arch	start	farm	card	sharp
yard	charm	smart	spark	bars
shark	star	chart	yarn	darts

or (Dictionaries indicate this sound as ōr.)

short	born	pork	storm	north
torch	cork	worn	port	corn
form	sport	lord	scorch	torn
stork	scorn	sort	thorn	porch
horn	fork	forth	morn	cord

r-Controlled Vowel Mix-Up

part	curve	storm	march	sport
skirt	under	darn	thorn	herd
born	harm	clerk	burn	short
flower	north	twirl	bark	worn
mark	church	father	dirty	smart

HARD AND SOFT C

Hard c

cave	class	catch	count	curb
crew	coat	deck	cool	cute
truck	cage	close	crash	cover
picnic	curve	picture	record	action

Soft c

cent	city	cinch	mice	center
space	lace	mince	cinder	peace
voice	twice	lacy	ace	since
rice	chance	place	cell	grace

Hard and Soft c Mix-Up

cymbal	acre	crest	receive	custom
process	choice	circle	active	attic
doctor	pencil	income	bicycle	recite
include	cried	decide	accept	dice

Hard and Soft c Mix-Up

circus	magic	descend	cycle	actor
parcel	mercy	rescue	deceive	select
country	discover	cypress	peacock	acid
recess	factory	actress	ceiling	force

HARD AND SOFT G

Hard g

glad	gripe	grow	gun	glove
game	good	goat	grace	gold
tag	hug	gang	glue	guide
goose	guard	twig	gone	gulf

Soft g

gem	gym	gin	bridge	magic
age	edge	badge	giant	genie
large	fudge	judge	urge	huge
strange	page	engine	agent	dodge

Hard and Soft g Mix-Up

hug	huge	garden	range	ground
shrug	ginger	larger	gentle	growl
energy	organ	garage	pigeon	agree
single	gulp	danger	disgrace	orange

Hard and Soft g Mix-Up

pygmy	general	manage	pigment	agent
strange	degree	struggle	giraffe	nudge
dogwood	garbage	package	against	gypsy
glory	stingy	rogue	signal	grand

FRIENDLY LETTER FORM

_____

_____

_____

_____

_____

_____

_____

_____

_____

_____

_____

CURSIVE ALPHABET

Outline Form

Subject: _____

   I. _____

      A. _____

      B. _____

      C. _____

  II. _____

      A. _____

      B. _____

      C. _____

 III. _____

      A. _____

      B. _____

      C. _____

         1. _____

         2. _____

SYLLABLES: COMPOUND WORDS

A compound word is divided between its short words. If one of these words has more than one syllable, that word is divided also. Have the child pronounce the words in each column, then fold the sheet lengthwise. Ask him to divide the words in the second column into syllables, then open the sheet and check his work.

side walk	sidewalk
rain coat	raincoat
out doors	outdoors
no where	nowhere
home sick	homesick
grand son	grandson
flash light	flashlight
corn cob	corncob
neck lace	necklace
light house	lighthouse
down stairs	downstairs
broad cast	broadcast
hair do	hairdo
name plate	nameplate
search light	searchlight
pig tails	pigtails
mush room	mushroom
pipe line	pipeline
pock et book	pocketbook
news pa per	newspaper
land own er	landowner
jack rab bit	jackrabbit
grass hop per	grasshopper

SYLLABLES: VC/CV

When two consonants come between two vowels, divide the word between the two consonants. Do not divide consonant blends or consonant digraphs; they are treated as if they were one consonant. Have the child pronounce the words in each column, then fold the sheet lengthwise. Ask him to divide the words in the second column into syllables, then open the sheet and check his work.

swim ming	swimming
cin der	cinder
chim ney	chimney
pic ture	picture
drop per	dropper
six ty	sixty
trac tor	tractor
ad mire	admire
plas tic	plastic
cur tain	curtain
pen cil	pencil
cir cus	circus
ab sent	absent
gob lin	goblin
in flate	inflate
or phan	orphan
sur prise	surprise
es cape	escape
far ther	farther
mer chant	merchant
an chor	anchor
king dom	kingdom
com plete	complete

SYLLABLES: V/CV

When a two-syllable word has one consonant between two vowels, if the first vowel is long it is divided before the consonant. Have the child pronounce the words in each column, then fold the sheet lengthwise. Ask him to divide the words in the second column into syllables, then open the sheet and check his work.

se cret	secret
ti ger	tiger
po lite	polite
la bel	label
cu pid	cupid
me ter	meter
li lac	lilac
pu pil	pupil
be gin	begin
mi nus	minus
pe can	pecan
tu lip	tulip
na ture	nature
stu pid	stupid
spi der	spider
lo cate	locate
pi lot	pilot
to tal	total
wa fer	wafer
ti dy	tidy
ze ro	zero
hu man	human
ra zor	razor
i tem	item

SYLLABLES: VC\V

When a two-syllable word has one consonant between two vowels, if the first vowel is short it is divided after the consonant. Have the child pronounce the words in each column, then fold the sheet lengthwise. Ask him to divide the words in the second column into syllables, then open the sheet and check his work.

drag on	dragon
sev en	seven
me lon	melon
tim id	timid
lem on	lemon
wag on	wagon
trav el	travel
cab in	cabin
pun ish	punish
met al	metal
cam el	camel
den im	denim
hab it	habit
mag ic	magic
shad ow	shadow
dam age	damage
rob in	robin
val ue	value
clev er	clever
ped al	pedal
com ic	comic
pal ace	palace
man age	manage
liv er	liver

SYLLABLES: V/CV AND VC/V MIX-UP

Have the child pronounce the words in each column, then fold the sheet lengthwise. Ask him to divide the words in the second column into syllables, then open the sheet and check his work. Talk about the reason for any error.

pi lot	pilot
lo cate	locate
drag on	dragon
mag ic	magic
nev er	never
cam el	camel
pun ish	punish
na ture	nature
se cret	secret
spi der	spider
pal ace	palace
tow el	towel
wa fer	wafer
ze ro	zero
lem on	lemon
la bel	label
pe can	pecan
mel on	melon
hu man	human
rob in	robin
po lite	polite
riv er	river
li lac	lilac
cab in	cabin

SYLLABLES: VC/CV, V/CV, AND VC/V MIX-UP

Have the child pronounce the words in the two columns, then fold the sheet lengthwise. Ask him to divide each word in the second column into syllables and record its rule on the blank beside it. Open the sheet and have him check his work. Talk about the reason for any error.

pic ture	picture	_____
com ic	comic	_____
pol ish	polish	_____
cu pid	cupid	_____
lo cate	locate	_____
chim ney	chimney	_____
pen cil	pencil	_____
cir cus	circus	_____
hab it	habit	_____
clos et	closet	_____
to tal	total	_____
met al	metal	_____
ze ro	zero	_____
com plete	complete	_____
trac tor	tractor	_____
wa fer	wafer	_____
man age	manage	_____
ra zor	razor	_____
den im	denim	_____
or phan	orphan	_____
o mit	omit	_____
prob lem	problem	_____
shad ow	shadow	_____

SYLLABLES: V/V

When a word has two vowels side-by-side that are sounded separately,
divide the word between the two vowels. This rule may be written as V/V.
Have the child pronounce the words in each column, then fold the sheet
lengthwise. Ask him to divide the words in the second column into syllables, then open the sheet and correct his work.

cre ate	create
pli ers	pliers
li on	lion
po em	poem
ru in	ruin
di et	diet
ri ot	riot
ra di o	radio
vi o lin	violin
the a ter	theater
an nu al	annual
i de al	ideal
vi o lets	violets
pi an o	piano
ro de o	rodeo
di a gram	diagram
cas u al	casual
grad u ate	graduate
di a mond	diamond
cam e o	cameo
po li o	polio

Syllables: VC/CV, V/CV, VC/V, and V/V Mix-Up

Have the child pronounce the words in the two columns, then fold the sheet lengthwise. Ask him to divide each word in the second column into syllables and record its rule on the blank beside it. Open the sheet and have him check his own work. Talk about the reason for any error.

cat nip	catnip	_____
gi ant	giant	_____
rob in	robin	_____
rap id	rapid	_____
di et	diet	_____
tab let	tablet	_____
e ven	even	_____
pic ture	picture	_____
vic tim	victim	_____
qui et	quiet	_____
ti ny	tiny	_____
com ic	comic	_____
pu pil	pupil	_____
fu ture	future	_____
po lite	polite	_____
ex tend	extend	_____
cab in	cabin	_____
prob lem	problem	_____
cre ate	create	_____
mag ic	magic	_____
doc tor	doctor	_____
pli ers	pliers	_____
val ue	value	_____

SUFFIXES AND WORD ENDINGS

Teach the child to spell each word ending. Do not assign these words for spelling lessons; use them to teach the child to spell by syllables. Pronounce a word and have the child repeat it. Say the word slowly, giving him time to write it syllable by syllable, then ask him to say the word again. When he has finished writing the words in a list, have him read aloud the words he just wrote.

en

chick en	chicken
froz en	frozen
short en	shorten
fright en	frighten
brok en	broken
a wak en	awaken
mis tak en	mistaken

ly

bare ly	barely
light ly	lightly
brave ly	bravely
proud ly	proudly
ex act ly	exactly
qui et ly	quietly
se cret ly	secretly

ful

pain ful	painful
bash ful	bashful
aw ful	awful
fright ful	frightful
won der ful	wonderful
de light ful	delightful
for get ful	forgetful

ment

tor ment	torment
state ment	statement
base ment	basement
mo ment	moment
ar gu ment	argument
de part ment	department
ex cite ment	excitement

_le

gen tle	gentle
ca ble	cable
set tle	settle
bun dle	bundle
fa ble	fable
jun gle	jungle

less

help less	helpless
taste less	tasteless
sight less	sightless
hope less	hopeless
care less	careless
pow er less	powerless

SUFFIXES AND WORD ENDINGS

Teach the child to spell each word ending. Do not assign these words for spelling lessons; use them to teach the child to spell by syllables.

est

fin est	finest
small est	smallest
wis est	wisest
long est	longest
hap pi est	happiest
hun gri est	hungriest
nois i est	noisiest

ture

pic ture	picture
na ture	nature
cap ture	capture
fix ture	fixture
pas ture	pasture
struc ture	structure
ad ven ture	adventure

tive

cap tive	captive
mo tive	motive
na tive	native
rel a tive	relative
at ten tive	attentive
de tec tive	detective
pos i tive	positive

ous

fa mous	famous
cu ri ous	curious
nu mer ous	numerous
se ri ous	serious
mar vel ous	marvelous
pre vi ous	previous
ob vi ous	obvious

ing

cloth ing	clothing
danc ing	dancing
mock ing	mocking
rid ing	riding
be long ing	belonging
de bat ing	debating
ex tend ing	extending
de mand ing	demanding

tion

men tion	mention
no tion	notion
sta tion	station
ac tion	action
ques tion	question
re la tion	relation
va ca tion	vacation
at ten tion	attention

PHONICS AND SYLLABLE RULES

1. There is a vowel sound in every syllable.

2. When there is only one vowel in a syllable, and it is followed by a consonant, that vowel is short.

3. If there is only one vowel in a syllable, and it is at the end of the syllable, that vowel is usually long. (This is often not true of the middle syllables.)

4. When there are two vowels in a syllable, the first vowel is usually long, and the second vowel is silent.

5. In the middle syllables of words, a single vowel may be short or long. The vowels **a, e, i, o,** and **u** very often have the schwa sound—the sound you hear in the **a** in around.

6. The r-controlled vowels **er, ir,** and **ur** have the sound you hear in her, bird, and fur. The **ar** usually has the sound you hear in far. The **or** usually has the sound you hear in for.

7. The diphthongs:
    oi and **oy** have the sound you hear in oil and boy.
    au and **aw** have the sound you hear in caught and yawn.
    ou and **ow** have the sound you hear in loud and cow.
    ew and **oo** have the sound you hear in new and moon.

8. The soft sounds of **c** and **g**:
    c has the sound of **s** if the next letter after it is **e, i,** or **y**, as in the words cent, city, and icy.
    g usually has the sound of **j** if the next letter after it is **e, i,** or **y**, as in the words gem, ginger, and gym.

9. **C** and **g** have their hard sound when they are not followed by **e, i,** or **y**. You hear their hard sounds in cake and glad.

SUFFIXES AND WORD ENDINGS: SYLLABLE RULES

Suffixes and Word Endings

ate	create	ly	quickly
cial	special	ment	moment
cious	precious	ness	kindness
ed	counted	sion	confusion
en	frozen	sive	expensive
er	braver	tain	certain
es	bushes	tial	initial
est	finest	tion	attention
ful	painful	tive	relative
ing	saying	ture	future
ion	fashion	ty	safety
ist	tourist	y	mystery
less	careless	_le	people

Rules for Dividing Words Into Syllables

1. A compound word is divided between its short words. If one of these words has more than one syllable, that word is divided also. Example: newspaper (news pa per).
2. When two consonants come between two vowels, divide the word between the two consonants (VC/CV). Example: admire (ad mire).
3. When a two-syllable word has one consonant between two vowels, if the first vowel is long, it is divided before the consonant (V/CV). Example: razor (ra zor).
4. When a two-syllable word has one consonant between two vowels, if the first vowel is short, it is divided after the consonant (VC/V). Example: manage (man age).
5. When a word has two vowels side-by-side that are sounded separately, divide the word between the two vowels (V/V). Example: diet (di et).

SYLLABLES

This sheet is for use in teaching the child how to divide words into syllables and spell them. Fold the sheet down the center lengthwise. After the child has pronounced the first column of words, ask him to turn the sheet over and separate the words into syllables. Have him open the sheet and check his work. Talk about the reason for any error; then use the list of words for spelling by syllables.

a gree ment	agreement
mi cro scope	microscope
tri an gle	triangle
e quip ment	equipment
di a gram	diagram
at ten tion	attention
mu se um	museum
ex am ple	example
in di cate	indicate
un der stand	understand
ar gu ment	argument
vol ca no	volcano
en vi ous	envious
sev er al	several
rel a tive	relative
ve hi cle	vehicle
il lus trate	illustrate
suc cess ful	sucessful
fab u lous	fabulous
how ev er	however
es tab lish	establish
de part ment	department
cu ri ous	curious

SYLLABLES

This sheet is to be used in teaching the child how to divide words into syllables and spell them.

de pos it	deposit
va ca tion	vacation
min er al	mineral
ex er cise	exercise
de tec tive	detective
sub trac tion	subtraction
ar ti cle	article
mar vel ous	marvelous
per fec tion	perfection
con tent ment	contentment
pre tend ed	pretended
cen tu ry	century
glo ri ous	glorious
con ver sa tion	conversation
grav i ty	gravity
ex act ly	exactly
ad ven ture	adventure
ob vi ous	obvious
plan ta tion	plantation
set tle ment	settlement
for get ful	forgetful
ex tend ed	extended
di vid ed	divided
hor i zon tal	horizontal
bi ol o gist	biologist

SYLLABLES

This sheet is to be used in teaching the child how to divide words into syllables and spell them.

ed u ca tion	education
as tron o mer	astronomer
i den ti fy	identify
em ploy er	employer
re mark a ble	remarkable
ad di tion al	additional
cre a tive	creative
qui et ness	quietness
el e ment	element
se cret ly	secretly
com fort a ble	comfortable
ex e cu tion	execution
tem per a ture	temperature
val u a ble	valuable
un im por tant	unimportant
con sec u tive	consecutive
ab so lute ly	absolutely
trans por ta tion	transportation
re la tion ship	relationship
ob serv a to ry	observatory
in ter sec tion	intersection
co op er a tive	cooperative
pub li ca tion	publication
con tin u ous	continuous
ex pla na tion	explanation

SYLLABLES

This sheet is to be used in teaching the child how to divide words into syllables and spell them.

dis ap point ment	disappointment
in dus tri al	industrial
hes i tat ed	hesitated
com men ta tor	commentator
mul ti pli ca tion	multiplication
in tel li gent	intelligent
par tic u lar	particular
con sid er a ble	considerable
ex per i ment ing	experimenting
no ti fi ca tion	notification
com mu ni cat ing	communicating
u ni ver si ty	university
news pa per man	newspaperman
or di nar y	ordinary
ra di o ac tive	radioactive
for ev er more	forevermore
o ver pow er	overpower
ques tion a ble	questionable
clas si fi ca tion	classification
in ter na tion al	international
civ i li za tion	civilization
not with stand ing	notwithstanding
un sat is fac to ry	unsatisfactory
me te o rol o gist	meteorologist
i den ti fi ca tion	identification

TUTOR'S WEEKLY LESSON PLAN GUIDE: PRIMER

Vocabulary:

Review the ten vocabulary words previously assigned by having the child shuffle their cards and say the words. If he hesitates while pronouncing them, mix the cards up and have him say them two more times. File those he knows under "(child's name) knows these."

Assign new words to be learned during the coming week, grouping them in order of appearance into two five-word groups. The words should be assigned so that they are mastered several days before the child first encounters them in the primer's story. If the child is unable to learn the vocabulary words fast enough, have him reread a favorite story to give him the time he needs to catch up.

Reading:

Check the child's reading comprehension by having him talk about the pictures on the pages he read during the past week.

The child is to use a strip of heavy paper (1½″ wide and 9″ long) when reading, placing it beneath the first line and sliding it down beneath each line as he reads. Read the story in this order:

1. Child reads aloud.
2. Tutor reads slowly with expression.
3. Child rereads aloud.
4. The child and tutor talk about what is happening in the story.

Phonics:

Ask the child to read the chart of short and long vowels.

Review any previously taught phonics fact the child seems not to be using.

If time permits, teach a new phonics fact.

Game Time:

At the end of each one-hour lesson, save ten minutes for a game that will strengthen or introduce a reading skill.

Planning Next Week's Homework:

On one side of a paper strip, list each day's reading assignment, planning homework that will take no more than thirty minutes.

Example:

Tues.	Fri.
p. 15, 16	p. 21, 22
Wed.	Sat.
p. 17, 18	p. 23, 24
Thurs.	Mon.
p. 19, 20	Tutor: 10:00

Tell the parent to drill on the vocabulary words one group at at time, having the child say the group's words three times during each lesson. The parent is to say each word as he or she lays the card down, then have the child repeat it. The child is not to be asked to sound it. If he hesitates trying to recall it, the parent should count from one to five silently, then say the word.

TUTOR'S WEEKLY LESSON PLAN GUIDE: FIRST GRADE

Vocabulary:

Review the ten vocabulary words previously assigned by having the child shuffle their cards and say the words. Mix the cards up and have him say the words again.

Check the book's vocabulary list by having him say the words that will first appear on one of the next fifteen pages. He will probably know some of them. File these words and those he has learned during the past week in his stack of words labeled "(child's name) knows these."

Assign the new words to be learned by grouping them in order into two, or at most three, five-word groups. If there are any words of more than one syllable, call the child's attention to how the syllables are separated.

Reading:

Talk about the story the child just finished. How did it end? Was it an interesting story? Why? Why not?

Have the child continue to slide a strip of heavy paper (1½" wide and 9" long) beneath each line as he reads. Read the story in this order:

1. Child reads aloud.
2. Tutor reads slowly with expression.
3. Child rereads story.
4. Child, in his own words, tells what is happening in the story. Child and tutor talk about it.

Phonics:

Review the sounds of long and short vowels.

Review previously taught phonics facts the child does not fully understand or seems not to be using.

Teach a new phonics fact.

Spelling and Writing:

Each week ask the child to learn to spell three or four words from the Most Used Words lists. Check and recheck the words he has been learning. With "invisible" writing he can print these with his finger on the tabletop.

Dictate two very short sentences made from words he has learned to spell. Have him write these on very wide-lined paper.

Game Time:

Save ten minutes at the end of his one-hour lesson for a game that will strengthen or introduce a reading skill.

Planning Next Week's Homework:

Homework lessons should be no more than thirty minutes long. At this level the child will probably be able to read one and one-half pages of sentences. This may be as much as three pages in his reader if half of each page is a picture. If two pages are filled with sentences, write "stop" in the middle of one page. If the vocabulary words are difficult, have him reread a favorite story. List his week's reading assignments on the back of a paper strip.

Example:

Thurs.	Tues.
p. 87–89	Reread p. 47–49
Fri.	Spelling Words: saw, have,
p. 90, 91	for
Sat.	Wed.
p. 91, 92	Tutor: 3:30
Mon.	
Reread p. 45, 46	

Tell the parent to teach the groups of vocabulary words. The child is to say the five words, mix them up, and say them two more times at the beginning of each lesson. At the end of that lesson, ask him to repeat the words he is having difficulty recalling.

Teach the child the three spelling words. Each day have him say the word, spell it orally, write it, then say it again.

TUTOR'S WEEKLY LESSON PLAN GUIDE: SECOND GRADE

Vocabulary:

Ask the child to shuffle and say the vocabulary words assigned to him the previous week. Have him say the list of vocabulary words that will first appear on one of the next fifteen pages of his reading book.

Group the words he does not know into two, or at most three, five-word groups to be learned during the coming week. File those he knows in his stack of words labeled "(child's name) knows these." Call the child's attention to the syllables in longer words.

Reading:

Ask the child to tell the most important things happening in the stories he read that week. The child should continue to slide a strip of heavy paper (1½″ wide and 9″ long) down beneath the lines as he reads, until he has no difficulty keeping his place. Read two or three pages each day in this order:

1. Child reads aloud.
2. He tells in detail what he has just read.
3. Tutor and child talk about it.
4. Child rereads the page aloud.

When the child's reading is becoming fairly smooth, have him read part of an easy page silently, tell in detail what happened, and reread the page orally.

Phonics and Reading Skills:

Ask the child to say the short- and long-vowel sounds and explain how he can tell whether the vowel in a word is short or long.

Review phonics facts that he hasn't mastered.

Teach phonics fact or a reading skill.

Spelling and Writing:

Check and recheck words from the Most Used Words lists. Assign five new words for his spelling lesson.

Ask him to write a short story (three or four sentences) during the coming week.

Game Time:

Save ten minutes at the end of his lesson for a game that strengthens or introduces a reading skill.

Planning Next Week's Homework:

Homework lessons should take no more than thirty minutes to complete. The child should write his short story at another time, with help only in spelling new words.

Write his reading assignments on the back of a paper strip.

Example:

Wed.	Mon.
p. 105, 106	p. 114–116
Thurs.	Spelling Words: own,
p. 107–109	draw, laugh, their, learn
Fri.	Tues.
p. 110, 111	Tutor: 3:30
Sat.	Bring story
p. 112, 113	

The parent is to teach the child the vocabulary words. If a change has been made in the child's reading order, explain why and how. Ask the parent to encourage the child to write the story with a minimum of help.

Tutor's Weekly Lesson Plan Guide: Third Grade

Vocabulary:

Shuffle the vocabulary cards and have the child say the words assigned the previous week. If he is very slow in recalling a word, assign it a second week.

Have him say the vocabulary words that will first appear on one of the next twenty pages. Tell him to look up unfamiliar words in the reading book's glossary or in the dictionary.

Group the words he does not know into two or three five-word groups. File those he knows in his stack of words labeled "(child's name) knows these."

Reading:

Ask the child how the story he just finished ended. Could he come up with a different ending?

Continue assigning oral reading until the child is able to recall vocabulary words easily, then have him read daily in this order:

1. Child reads silently.
2. He tells in detail what he has just read.
3. Tutor and child talk about the story.
4. Child rereads one page orally.

Syllabication and Spelling:

Teach the child a syllabication rule. Have him divide a list of words into syllables and help him correct the list. Review the syllabication and phonics rules involved.

Do not give him this list to study. Pronounce some of its words for him to spell. Tell him to think about their syllables as he writes them.

Ask him to memorize the spellings of five suffixes.

Reading Skills:

Assign three pages in a workbook to be done at home during the week. Make sure the child reads and understands the directions.

Writing:

Think up a different ending for the story he is to read on p. 85–90 in his reader and write a paragraph about it in cursive writing.

Game Time:

Save time for a game that will strengthen a phonics or syllabication skill.

Planning Next Week's Homework:

On nights that his school assigns homework, the child's lesson should be no longer than thirty minutes. In the summertime his daily lessons should be longer—one forty-five minute session or two thirty-minute sessions.

Write his reading assignments on a sheet of paper.

Example:

Tues.	Sat.
p. 85–87	p. 96, 97
	Spelling:
Wed.	-tion, -ous, -age,
p. 88–90	-ture, -cious
Thurs.	Mon.
p. 91, 92	Tutor: 4:00
Fri.	
p. 93–95	

The parent is to teach the child the vocabulary words and suffixes and encourage him to write the paragraph with a minimum of help. If there is too much homework for any one night, read two pages that night instead of three.

Appendix

For one-to-one tutoring, try to choose readers the child will enjoy. Except for assigned homework, it is best not to use the child's schoolbooks. Other good basic readers and phonics workbooks are available. Your school may be able to supply you with readers that are not being used in its classrooms. If they cannot, go to the public library; you will find basic readers on their shelves. Select a series at the child's reading level. If the library is unable to lend you a book for an extended time, you or your school can usually order it.

Addresses of publishers frequently change. The publisher named in the book may be a subsidiary of a large corporation, or the book may now be published by a different company. Ask the library's reference division for the publisher's current address and telephone number. When you phone the publisher, ask for their school division.

You can purchase phonics workbooks at school supply stores or from school book publishers.

The *Victory Drill Book* mentioned in Part One of this book contains seventy-two lists of words arranged in a proper order for teaching phonics. Its publisher's address is: Victory Drill Book, 501 Pecan Way, La Habra, CA 90631.

Listed below are a few of the publishers' names you will find in good basic readers:

Harcourt Brace & Co.
6277 Sea Harbor Dr.
Orlando, FL 32887

D. C. Heath & Co.
125 Spring St.
Lexington, MA 02173

Holt Rinehart & Winston, Inc.
1120 S. Capital of Texas Hwy.
No. 11-1100
Austin, TX 78746

Houghton Mifflin Co.
222 Berkeley St.
Boston, MA 02116

The Macmillan Co.
100 Tappan Rd.
Old Tappan, NJ 07675

McGraw-Hill Co.
1221 Ave. of the Americas
New York, NY 10020

Science Research Associates
220 E. Danieldale Rd.
DeSoto, TX 75115-2490

Scotts Foresman & Co.
1900 East Lake Ave.
Glenview, IL 60025

Silver Burdette & Ginn, Inc.
250 James St., East Div.
Morristown, NJ 07962